NAKED
AT THE
KNIFE-
EDGE

NAKED
AT THE
KNIFE-
EDGE

WHAT EVEREST TAUGHT ME
ABOUT LEADERSHIP AND THE
POWER OF VULNERABILITY

VIVIAN
JAMES RIGNEY

Forefront
BOOKS

NAKED AT THE KNIFE-EDGE
What Everest Taught Me about Leadership
and the Power of Vulnerability

© 2022 by Vivian James Rigney

Published by Forefront Books.

Cover Design by Bruce Gore, Gore Studios, Inc.
Interior Design by Mary Sue Oleson, BLU DESIGN CONCEPTS

ISBN: 9781637630778 print
ISBN: 9781637630785 e-book

CONTENTS

Acknowledgments

MY PARENTS, Séamus and Mary, raised five boys and set an example for each of us. Hard work, education, and family were their ethos, and it pervaded everything—to live and develop oneself with purpose. It was especially good to share my writing and have them be part of the journey creating this memoir. My dad passed away before the book was complete, and the immense sadness and emotions that arose from this shock brought much into perspective. Today, I hike with his love of mountains, wildlife, nature, and Ireland in my DNA. Mum, you have always been my greatest supporter and you continue to inspire me—every single day.

To my brothers—Paul, whose memory was with me in spirit every day on Everest and who diluted my fears and allowed me to find peace. Ivan, who has been an inspiration and a tower of strength during the past year, despite the challenges. Patrick and Ronan, who are the best big brothers one could have—kind, generous, supportive, and always glass-half-full. And of course, their wives and each of my twelve endlessly talented nieces and nephews, who broaden the love and perspectives within the family.

To the team—I was incredibly fortunate to be supported by an exceptional guiding company, Mountain Trip, that is truly world-class. My Everest guides, Scott Woolums and Bill Allen, helped create a unique team mindset, which matched safety with individual and team responsibility and connection, and for this I am forever grateful. I am grateful to my climbing colleagues, Ania Lichota, Cindy Abbott, and Paul and Denise Fejtek, who helped create a camaraderie that sustained me and lightened the tougher days with wit, humor, and humanity, although I was at greatest risk from cracking my ribs with laughter.

To our Sherpa, who were pillars of strength and courage throughout and whose humility and humor will forever stay with me, including Dawa Sherpa, Da Ongchhu Sherpa, Temba Sherpa, Karma Sherpa, Passing Sherpa, Tarke Sherpa, Passang Gomba Sherpa, Sonam Sherpa, Sange Sherpa, Pem Sherpa, Pem Chhotar Sherpa, Da Kusang Sherpa, Perba Surki Sherpa, Mingma Sherpa, Da Phinju Sherpa, Mindu Sherpa, and Ongdi Sherpa. And especially Gomba, who led me upward from the South Summit and, eventually, to the top of the world.

To The Green Monks, a small Irish hiking group founded by my father and his closest friends more than sixty years ago, which introduced hiking as very much a family sport and still introduces new generations to the supremely beautiful mountains and highlands of Ireland.

This book would not have been possible without the wisdom and guidance of many. Thank you to my good friends Kate McKay, Shirley Chan, Susan Macgregor-Scott, and Dave Dempsey for your insights, feedback, and patience. Your belief in the purpose of this book, and helping to bring my full self to writing it, was a huge motivation for me. And indeed, for the many others—you know who you are—who were my counsel and kitchen cabinet throughout the journey.

Finally, a special thanks to the team that helped me bring this book to publication: to Christina Boys and also Courtney Luzzi for their detailed, thoughtful, and thorough editing at different stages of writing, and to Owen Fitzpatrick, who generously shared his experience and wisdom as an accomplished writer and motivated me to just get on with it!

Go raibh maith agaibh go léir.

NEW YORK CITY, MAY 2021

Introduction

THE WIND WAS BITING. My lungs were bone-dry, heaving effort with each inhalation, but there was no air.

Our lead guide, Scott, leaned against a rock, green-faced with eyes bulging. "I don't think I can do it, I don't think I can summit. I'm not feeling good . . . "

"Vivian, are you okay?" Bill, our other guide, shouted across the howling wind as he slowly passed. His mouth hung open like a sagging drawbridge and his distant eyes were squinting through the blowing ice crystals.

"No air, Bill, no air!" I replied.

Our small team had just reached the South Summit of Mount Everest, better known as the false summit. Hillary Step filled my entire vista—an endless, almost vertical wall of jagged rock smothered intermittently by angled, wind-sculpted ice cornices. Outlines of distant climbers, like ants against the imposing rock, hauled their exhausted bodies up on a single rope. Between me and Hillary Step was a knife-edge ridge, about one boot-width across that I would need to walk along. On either side was pure air—thousands of meters falling away in both directions—Nepal to the left, Tibet to the right.

11

Suddenly I could not move. The remaining vestiges of energy in my body rapidly hemorrhaged away. I was unable to wake, not from a nightmare but from reality, which was infinitely worse. We had climbed for almost two months *on* the mountain to get to this point.

What if I don't survive this? What if I never make it off this mountain? The cold grew as fear filled me, followed by intense and piercing loneliness. The horizon darkened as a cloud grew over my head. The tears that welled up in my eyes instantly froze my eyelids shut as the elements attacked me from all sides.

"Why are you here?" The unfamiliar voice came from deep inside me with a piercing tone. *"Why are you trying to prove how good you are? How smart you are? How accomplished you are?"*

It grew louder. *"Why are you here?"*

Its pure, unadulterated judgment stripped me bare. I felt like a fraud. Yet I could not change my reality—I was here.

"Why are you here?"

I had no answer.

I would die leaning against this rock with this reckoning filling my head until my last breath.

I had never felt so alone in my entire life.

As leaders, how many times have we felt like this? How many times have we been in a situation where we felt trapped, overwhelmed, and alone with our own thoughts and emotions? It is this loneliness that has led me to write this book—a loneliness that most of us feel in different forms throughout our lives yet rarely speak about publicly. It's as if there's a shame associated with it.

Sometimes it's crystal clear, but oftentimes it's a subtle feeling that is quickly smothered by distractions, reactions, and impulses that pull us in one direction or another. Rarely is it explored and unpacked so that we reveal its core, what's causing it, and what can be distilled into a valid resolution. Perhaps the biggest anesthetic is our ambition and inner drive, which, while lauded in the corporate world, can be equally at odds with smart, effective, and emotionally intelligent awareness and leadership. And though we can achieve great success externally, we may be living in great denial internally.

Climbing the world's greatest summits, I learned not only about leadership but about the summits inside ourselves. As much as Everest is a team sport, with a huge reliance on climbing colleagues and support teams, the biggest mountain is within us. Nobody can carry you up Everest. You are fully accountable for your own journey. People think the ascent is a momentous physical challenge, which it clearly is, but it is much more than that. **It is the mind that allows a summit to happen.** And this same mind unravels quickly and relentlessly when drive and determination become evidently hollow attributes on their own. Our insatiable appetite for achievement ultimately leads to a place in which we don't know where or who we are in life. It's often referred to as "imposter syndrome." The ego, what we want to believe about ourselves, and the persona, what we want others to believe about us—two core pillars of education and conditioning—quickly become undone, revealing our true inner selves.

Many compelling books about climbing tall mountains tell detailed and insightful stories about the physical challenges. This one will seek a different route. Reflecting on my experience as an individual and as an executive coach working with business leaders around the world, I'll show how Everest serves as a powerful metaphor whereby vulnerability and leadership are inexorably linked.

Climbing Mount Everest taught me more about myself than anything I had done in my entire life up to that point. I had to find a way both to let go and move forward in order to survive, which is an intrinsically difficult thing to do *in the moment*. What I learned from the experience is one of the things that inspires me to do the work I do today. My specialty requires me to help people find their own Everest—their own true north—and in doing so, harness the best of themselves. It's not easy. It's a hard process, and life throws all kinds of obstacles in the way. But it's a journey to be traveled, and if I can do it, *you can do it too*.

PART 1

FROM SKYSCRAPERS TO BASE CAMP

CHAPTER 1

AVOIDANCE

I LET OUT A ROAR and sat upright in my bed, eyes wide open and still half asleep. The sweat poured off my forehead. A searing picture ran through my mind: my bare feet on Everest, frozen solid, the paleness of the skin punctured by black rims of frostbite encasing all my toes. I could feel the cold and the pain as it reverberated up from my extremities.

I rubbed my face with hands shaking uncontrollably and walked into my living room. The relative quiet of the Manhattan skyline at 4:00 a.m. calmed me. In the guest bedroom, I gazed over my climbing and expedition gear, all neatly laid out and ready for final packing into duffel bags. I would be leaving for Nepal within forty-eight hours.

Everest, the seventh and final peak of the Seven Summits I'd faced—the highest peak on all seven continents of the planet. Everest, the culmination of fourteen years of expeditions and preparation. I had always said I'd climb six of the seven summits but never Everest. I innately believed Everest was beyond my capacity—too steep, too dangerous, too many obstacles that could not be planned for, not to mention the amount of time, training, and money needed to disappear from my work life for at least two months. Who was I to be climbing this mountain? I felt truly out of my league just thinking about it.

I was brought into the world of mountains by my father while growing up in Ireland. He was passionate about the great outdoors, and hitting the hills was his way to unwind after a long week at work. As a child, I didn't share the same passion and preferred to be at home doing warmer things or spending time just being a kid and playing with friends. At Sunday Mass, while those around me were praying for the repose of souls and world peace, my little hands were firmly clasped together praying for rain. That was when my mother would put her foot down and overrule the excursions. It's funny that once I grew up and left Ireland, those memories of being cold and uncomfortable were superimposed by memories of family, time spent with them and of missing them. In building my career around the world, mountains became escapes where I, too, could find space to unwind and appreciate who I was and where I came from.

It began when I was a young man living and working in Johannesburg, South Africa. I had a business trip to Tanzania coming up, and Mount Kilimanjaro was just a short hopper flight from Dar es Salaam. As an invincible twenty-six-year-old who didn't know much apart from drive and ambition, I decided to give it a go, despite my severe fear of heights. The folly of youth. I made it to the top and experienced the invisible barrier of altitude for the very first time. I became acutely aware of the disconnect between mind and body—my mind and fitness level were ready, but my lungs and body had something else to say.

On that climb, soaring above the plains of East Africa, I met a group of other climbers from Europe who were talking about the Seven Summits. And so the idea took root: an intriguing way to push myself physically beyond my comfort zone and perceived capability as well as a unique excuse to travel to and experience all seven continents on the planet. My father had summited Kilimanjaro and Mont Blanc when I was a teenager, so if I am honest with myself, underneath it all, undoubtedly, was also an unconscious need to prove myself to him and my family: that I, the shy young guy who left Ireland when I was twenty years old, was capable of equally high achievement and even surpassing it. It's these unconscious drivers from our childhood that control so much of who we are, if we allow them.

Over the next ten years I climbed five more of the peaks.

I attempted Aconcagua in Argentina (South America) in 2004, but I failed to reach the summit. On Day 17, pounded by 200 kmh (125 mph) winds and with food and tents destroyed around us, we had to retreat down the mountain with the peak in sight.

Elbrus (Europe) involved a two-week trip to the Russian Caucasus region in 2005—as much a geopolitical adventure as a physical one. The ascent was strenuous but steady, apart from a very cold summit day. We witnessed some other teams with badly prepared and ill-equipped climbers suffering from exhaustion and frostbite, which was a disturbing experience.

Denali in Alaska (North America) the following year was in effect a mini-Everest in terms of technical and weather-related challenges. My fear of heights was truly challenged here. We withstood a long and punishing 55-degree headwall (an almost vertical wall of ice) with fixed lines, unstable ice fields, and crevasse valleys, together with highly exposed knife-edge ridges.

In 2007 I summited Carstensz Pyramid in Indonesia

(Oceania), a highly technical climb involving rock-climbing skills, which I learned and honed in the Catskill Mountains near New York City. At one section, an earthquake years before had broken off part of a ridge, and we had to attach ourselves to a rope and, in an upside-down and flat position, pull ourselves across the gaping hole and 500 meters (1,650 feet) of air below.

Vinson Massif, in Antarctica, was a wonderous two-week adventure in 2008 to one of the most extreme and hard-to-reach places on earth. A small plane dropped us off on an exposed glacier from where we pulled 70-kilo (150 pounds) sleds for three days, carrying our full supplies to get to Base Camp for the climb. Weather-impacted travel delays and an explosive storm at high camp pinned us down for days.

In 2009, I made a second attempt at Aconcagua. The weather gods were with us; this time we reached the summit in just ten days. I had been stretched beyond my limits on each of the summits, and each mountain represented uniquely different challenges. My fear of heights was ever present and created much discomfort both leading up to and during the expeditions, where I had to face it. I had dug deep and learned to live with the fear while trying to balance the energy it sapped in the process. I believe a fear of heights is real and something you are born with. It does get better through resolute practice in calming the mind, but once you are back in normal life the fear resets itself, and you have to start all over again during a new climb. But that fear did not stop me from climbing another mountain.

So what was truly holding me back in attempting Everest? I had gained confidence from my experiences and had broken through many mental and physical barriers. But Everest was beyond comparison with the other summits—a vertical ultramarathon with wildly steep and exposed sections, innumerable obstacles and uncontrollables, topped off with an ever-increasing list of failed expeditions and deaths that numbered in the hundreds. My intuition told me that Everest was its own force—a mountain not to be reckoned with but rather one to be negotiated with, the climbers representing the subservient party.

Still, maybe, just maybe, I would consider it. While in Antarctica I had met Scott Woolums, a guide who was planning an expedition from the south side of Everest through Nepal in 2010. This would be Scott's fifth summit of Everest—a level of achievement that induced multiple questions of curiosity around the what, how, and when. His answers were consistent with my thinking: that it's a highly challenging mountain with great risk. He was clear that the expedition he was planning would be small in number but nimble and agile, and he would be handpicking his climbing team. I could tell he was a man of detail and process—harder to discern was how he would lead a team under the unique pressures of Everest.

Life seems to be a river of challenges and opportunities, and one way to handle them is for the human mind to get busy so you don't have to think too much. This busyness is a great anesthetic for not having to come to terms with doing something you fear or that causes anxiety. Within a few weeks of returning from Antarctica I was in touch with the climbing company, Mountain Trip, through which Scott would be leading the expedition. I completed the paperwork and wired my hefty deposit for the 2010 Everest expedition. It was a classic case of ambition superseding reason and intuition.

The next fourteen months were mostly about training and getting fit.

I have always been fit, so I amped my regime up about 20 percent to stretch myself without risking any training injuries. This entailed a mix of gym work, running, and swimming. One of my good friends, Dan McHugh, is an ultramarathon runner, and I was particularly lucky to train with him in Central Park on weekends. He has incredible drive, focus, and, above all, discipline. Dan broke down his training into a system of priorities combined with consistency. Even though physically I knew I would be ready, it's rarely fitness that carries you through Everest. Everyone on my team would be committed, disciplined, focused, and in great shape. The reality is that 70 percent mental focus versus 30 percent physical focus is what allows you to be in a position to attempt the summit.

I was navigating an exceptionally busy work schedule. I had come to the United States and as an entrepreneur started my own executive coaching consulting business just three years prior. Eighteen months after I arrived, the financial crisis of September 2008 hit. I rapidly had to rethink and reinvent my offering in line with the massive fault lines appearing in corporate America. The job market cratered while corporate restructuring went through a seismic transformation. It was a period of immense challenge, and the delicate economic recovery in 2010 was still very much a work in progress.

One operations leader at a large client, an American multinational bank, laid it all out: "Vivian, let me be raw and blunt with you; we are in turmoil right now. Amid the economic chaos, we have restructured and layers of management have been stripped out. The surviving executive leaders and managers have much larger responsibilities and expectations to deliver, without the resources and with demotivated teams. More burden on the shoulders of fewer leaders—the pancaking effect. Add in the immense new scrutiny from regulators on every aspect of our business, past and present, and we are at risk of leaders either giving up and fleeing or being unable to make decisions, like deer in the headlights. Our demise is a real possibility.

"Why you are here is that we believe this is a transformation opportunity, a must-change path. We believe in our leaders and we need them to believe in themselves and to act, lead, and execute. We are investing in executive coaching to give them support and head space to internalize this, each to their own needs. If you deliver results, we will remember you. If you don't, we will never work with you again."

The message was stark but authentic. And I respected it—a lot. This typifies the work I do and the people I work with. They are smart, driven, ambitious, and most often, lonely. Sitting high on the hierarchy, responsibilities lie on their shoulders and they have few people with whom to share their worries, concerns, and insecurities, so they tend to internalize their burdens, stresses, and vulnerabilities. Since intellectual energy is a finite resource, any unnecessary drain or waste can have exponential impact on decision-making, reading situations, and managing people effectively.

My training was a healthy distraction from this environment and helped me focus on what was physically awaiting me. It also put things in perspective: success on Everest meant avoiding death and coming home alive. A binary but sobering reality. It was a careful balancing act to carve out the time and pull myself out of bed to train well before dawn most mornings, but the resulting endorphins and fitness transformation sustained my intellectual energy levels. Running alone in Central Park under the streetlights also provided lots of time to think and solve—driving me to be more creative, more challenging of the status quo, and more open overall to my work as an executive coach.

The months passed, and the more people became aware of my ambition, the more they asked about it. I resolutely avoided going into details. In fact, I could feel myself beginning to block out the questions in my own mind. Friends and clients started referring to movies and documentaries on TV about Everest expeditions and asked whether I had seen them. My answer was always "not yet," which must have created a head-scratch about how nonchalantly I was approaching the trip. Here's a guy going to climb a scary mountain and he hasn't even bothered to watch anything or read up on it.

The truth was very different though—I was terrified just thinking about how I would handle the heights and get through it. I knew of the famous book *Into Thin Air* by John Krakauer, which describes in graphic detail the disaster of the 1996 Everest season when a violent storm on a packed summit day killed some of the world's most experienced guides and their climbing clients. There was also a slew of Discovery Channel–type documentaries about the mountain, again highlighting the ever-present danger and risks involved through the eyes of actual climbing teams. I didn't want my subconscious mind to start spinning around the dangers, so I simply blocked it out. Fear suppression was maximized with impressive efficiency. I limited my mind aperture to believing that I would be fit and driven enough to handle the obstacles—taking them one day at a time on the mountain. Avoidance and denial can take you only so far. It's something I had become good at—ploughing ahead fearlessly toward my goals and avoiding anything that might raise concerns or detract from them. When I was younger, it didn't matter as much—sheer drive paid me back in spades, and achievement soon followed. Yet for Everest, where the scale of the goal was so large and the risk so high, my avoidance of any books, video clips, or reports about the climb itself was a poor and ultimately futile strategy.

One incident punctured this cocoon of compartmentalization. One month before leaving New York, I was sent a form that required me to sign waivers ahead of the climb. It was titled "Body Disposal and Repatriation" and stated the following:

> *If you die on the mountain above 7,800 meters (25,590 ft), your body will be left at that location.*
>
> *If you die on the mountain above 5,300 meters (17,390 ft), your body may be put in a crevasse and possibly marked with a rock or cairn in a respectful manner by an expedition team member.*
>
> *If you die lower on the mountain, it may be possible to get your body down, where it could be cremated by the locals. This will cost several thousand dollars, including the cost of recovery labor, transport and body preparation, wood, and appropriate donations to the local monastery. This cost is usually between $5,000 and $10,000. It will not be possible to bring your ashes home due to the cremation process.*
>
> *If you die lower down on the mountain or on the trek to Base Camp, it may be possible to get your body down for repatriation to your country of residence. If you elect repatriation of your body, it would be via helicopter and would be quite complicated and expensive, and might take several weeks.*

Climbing tall mountains is inherently dangerous. It's not that climbers don't think of bad things happening and the risks associated with the sport—of course we do. But it is an implied risk, one that comes to the fore in real time when negotiating a knife-edge ridge, encountering a rockfall, or sharing experiences with fellow climbers on the mountain. This single document blew all that out into the open in a brief but unnervingly direct statement of scenarios. These facts had to be processed and understood by me alone before making my choices.

Anxiety flooded my conscious mind for the first time since signing up for the expedition. What would I want done with my body? What would be the impact on my family and my loved ones? What would I leave behind if something happened to me, and what would my legacy be? This theme would open up dramatically on the mountain, spinning me into dark and unfamiliar places. But I didn't know that then. I checked my preferences, signed, and returned the document, my busyness still a lifeline to distraction.

I had plenty of other things to occupy my mind. Taking a sabbatical from my own business for two months was unfamiliar territory for me; it felt like the game Whac-A-Mole in the week leading up to departure. There was a lot of contingency planning and client communication to ensure the company stayed on track and people were looked after. After that restless night the day before departure, with bags finally packed and zipped, I took one last walk through the city I loved. It was a perfect spring day in late March, and unseasonal warmth brought New Yorkers out of their apartments to fill the green expanses of Central Park. The leaves were not yet on the trees, but people had ecstatic looks on their faces, aware that winter was finally in full retreat and summer was beckoning. I strolled through the lawn in the Sheep Meadow. All these people were experiencing their structured day-to-day lives, which would continue for the next two months, whereas I was embarking into the abyss on an adventure that had limitless uncertainty and unknowns.

I felt a deep sense of appreciation marred only by a hint of loss in leaving my grounded life. I was unable to fully visualize (and internalize) what was ahead. Busyness had proven a highly effective distraction for me. But this strategy would return to haunt me over a month later when I faced the mountain and, above all, myself.

CHAPTER 2

DISCOVERING THE TEAM

I WAS FINALLY ON MY WAY. I had hauled two massive duffel bags, a large backpack, and a carry-on into a cab and taken one final glance over my shoulder at Manhattan slowly fading into the distance as we passed over the Queensboro Bridge, the iron struts and metalwork whizzing by.

As I waited for my flight at JFK, I opened my email and saw a message from Mountain Trip about one of our Everest guides, Heidi Kloos. Heidi had been a guide on my expedition to Antarctica just over a year before. She was inclusive, decisive, resourceful, and empathetic—innately knowing when to push and when to support—representing some of the key qualities for a mountaineering leader.

According to the email, she had set out from her home a few days ago for an afternoon ice climb, accompanied by her dog Menke. When she didn't return the following day, friends alerted Search and Rescue, who found her dog, her backpack, and one ski amid a mass of avalanche debris. An avalanche had killed her fiancée ten years before, and Heidi was known for having a very conservative approach to moving in avalanche terrain. As night fell, the rescue party had to descend the mountain, but her dog refused to leave with them and remained at the site overnight. The following afternoon they recovered her body, buried under several meters of snow. The north-facing slope where she was located was largely known to be safe and unexposed. It's believed she was ascending on skis when an overhang of snow and ice from a cliff above broke off and she was encased with debris.

The news stunned me. I could still hear her voice and infectious laugh in my head as I recalled the almost three weeks we spent together in Chile and Antarctica. She was an avid nature lover, and I remember her being enthralled looking at the penguins near Punta Arenas in Patagonia. Her assured leadership style was totally disarmed by these waddling birds, and in its place were sheer wonderment and childhood curiosity. She was one of the strongest climbers I have been on an expedition with. Experienced, confident, humble, and safe, Heidi was mentally and physically strong and someone who was living her dream. It felt impossible for her vibrant spirit to be extinguished within seconds. I felt my own emotions bubbling within me around her loss. I knew I would have to somehow emotionally prepare for the journey ahead by making peace with all the uncontrollables and the fears that came with the climb.

My flight routing was JFK to Delhi before connecting on to Kathmandu. About twelve hours into the flight, the captain made an announcement encouraging those who were awake to take a peek out of the left side of the plane. I rubbed my eyes and raised the shade. In the distance, the entire vista was taken over by a silhouette of Everest, the mountain I would start climbing in just a matter of days. I checked the screen—the Boeing 777 plane was close to its cruise altitude, almost 10 vertical kilometers (6.2 miles) above sea level, making it all the more imposing knowing that Everest itself is 8,848 meters, almost 5.5 miles tall. I had struck up a conversation with the American Airlines crew earlier, and they came over and wanted to chat, eyes full of excitement and wonder about the expedition as we all peered out in awe of the sight before us. I played along, but inside it felt surreal. I could feel the anxiety building within me.

We landed in Delhi around midnight, and I made the best of my last hours of high-speed Wi-Fi hunkered at the desk rather than sleeping at the SAS Radisson Hotel before my 6:30 a.m. flight to Nepal.

Kathmandu was a sensory feast. Nepal has never been colonized, which is unique for much of Asia. Arriving early in the morning, the cab ride to my hotel set the scene—haphazard with busy, winding, and dusty roads. The driver navigated around gaping potholes the size of small craters on the way to a bustling city of 1.5 million people. Just two years before, in 2008, a Maoist insurgency had led to the overthrow of an unpopular monarchy and to a huge political transformation. Now, despite leading the new government, Maoist supporters in red bandanas weaved through the traffic, whistling and demanding change. I was witnessing real-time nation-building and political adolescence as we snaked through the crowds on unmarked roads.

After a couple of hours, the taxi arrived at the Yak & Yeti Hotel in the center of Kathmandu. With wooden paneling and open verandas that led to a large garden of lush green lawns and huge trees, it was like something out of a Hemingway novel—a true oasis in the center of the bustling, dry, and polluted city. This hotel is an institution in Nepal and has been ground zero for many Everest expeditions, including that of Edmund Hillary and Tenzing Norgay in 1953.

Although my body felt leaden with jet lag, as I walked through the lobby and started to take it all in, I got a second wind of energy and quickly dropped my bags in my room. Pulling off my jeans and replacing them with shorts and flip-flops, I walked out into the bustling streets and chaotic exhilaration that is Kathmandu. It was like traveling back in time into an *Indiana Jones* movie. The streets were teeming with people dressed in vibrant colors of saffron, indigo, marigold, and emerald, and a cacophony of different noises, incredible smells, and domesticated animals greeted me in every direction. Street food redolent with ginger and spices wafted through the narrow lanes and alleys. The buzz of overladen trucks and motorbikes mixed with the bells of rickshaw vendors navigating their paths through the crowds, while chickens squawked in wooden cages. Nepal is a country with more than one hundred different ethnic groups speaking ninety-two different languages, a true social tapestry compressed into a relatively small land area, surrounded by the Himalayas. Thick smog hangs over the city, hiding the mountains and resulting in many hiker and climber tourists wearing masks to avoid picking up a lung infection. In a sense, I imagined it as an earlier version of New York City—without the concrete.

The people of Nepal were friendly, warm, and industrious, yet the poverty was overwhelming: beggars were on most street corners, many of them young children—their tiny faces beaming smiles and a few words of English to secure a few rupees. One young girl, no more than four years old, came up and gently tugged my sleeve. She was barefoot with tangled and matted hair, dressed in a torn T-shirt and shorts.

Her bright eyes gleamed up at me from her small and dusty face. Up to that point, I tried to avoid making eye contact as there were so many outstretched hands wherever you walked, but this girl was unavoidable. She didn't have an empty hand but instead offered me a small Hindu prayer card depicting a god with a halo around his head, offering a hand of peace.

"Hello, how are you, sir! Welcome!" she exclaimed.

"Hi, what a nice card. What's your name?" I replied.

She was silent.

"How old are you?"

She stared back at me. Both of us were paralyzed for those moments. She didn't know any English other than the few words she shared. I saw a child with all the innocence and dreams I had at her age. Yet her life path—living on the streets of Kathmandu—was and would be so surreally different and difficult compared to mine. I bought her card and tucked it tightly into my pocket. It would come with me up Everest.

Around every corner was a new sight, smell, or experience. The temples were ubiquitous, as were the people going about their normal daily lives. There was cooking on the street and the washing of clothes against scrubbing rocks in great squares, while cows roamed unencumbered through the streets. As a majority Hindu and thus mostly vegetarian country, the Nepalese consider cows to be a sacred symbol of life that should be revered and protected.

I turned a corner and stumbled into a large open square with a line of what looked like stone platforms. Some of them were smoldering, while others were stacked with wood and straw and topped with blossoms. I couldn't figure out what it was, so I waited for a few minutes and noticed a small group arrive carrying a body wrapped in a colorful sarong. I quickly realized that this was the square where the dead were publicly cremated in the presence of their families. Even though there were many random people standing around, it felt like an extremely private event, and I turned away and left.

Our group assembled for the first time that evening in the hotel. As we sat in the wide, plaid lounge chairs, Bill Allen introduced us. Bill was one of the owners of Mountain Trip, a highly respected guiding company from Telluride, Colorado. I was lucky enough to have been on expeditions that Bill led in Antarctica and Indonesia, and I felt privileged to have him as one of our guides on Everest. Bill would be supporting Scott, our lead guide, whose depth of experience on Everest was crucial to the planning, management, and leadership of the expedition. One of Bill's responsibilities was interviewing and assessing each prospective climber well in advance and deciding if they would be a good fit for the expedition. Experience climbing at altitude, use of crampons (boot spikes) on snow and ice, level of fitness, and being on a mountain for extended periods were all assessed. In addition, Bill considered how personalities, attitude, and sense of collective spirit would fit within a team. There was no guarantee that we would all make it to attempt the summit, but we needed to start from the best base possible.

Among the climbers were Paul and Denise Fejtek, a highly athletic couple from Southern California who were also attempting Everest as their seventh and final summit. Paul was climbing on behalf of the Challenged Athletes Foundation, as he had a birth injury limiting the use of his right arm. I already knew Ania Lichota, a Polish national working in banking in London. We had spent almost two weeks together in Antarctica, and I found her a determined and fun climbing colleague with a laugh that could pierce through the harshest storm. Cindy Abbott, a university professor from Southern California, had less high-altitude experience but had climbed with our head guide, Scott, previously. She was warm and extremely determined.

The hardest part of joining any climbing team is getting to know your fellow climbers—understanding and assessing who the introverts and extroverts are, the size of egos and personas, and all the idiosyncrasies of people that come to the surface as you spend time together. It's hard because it's natural to have a lot in common with some people and less so with others. Some people will make you laugh hard, while others will test your limits of patience and energy. What is important is that we all get along and that there's an openness to get to know and understand each other. Under times of extreme weather, stress, and unforeseen drama, we need to be able to count on one another—our lives may depend on it. We didn't have a choice in picking the people we would be sharing our lives with over the next two months. We entrusted Mountain Trip to do this for us, but on this evening, as we left the hotel to share our first of many meals together, we were acutely aware of getting to know with whom we would be putting our lives in danger on the mountain ahead of us.

We were very clearly warned in our first meeting about the high risk of picking up a bug in Kathmandu and then spending the rest of the trip fighting it at altitude—an exhausting and depleting process. One crucial lesson when climbing in faraway places is how sensitive human bodies and immune systems are to a change in environment. What was perfectly healthy for locals could be a problem for us. We were all super fit and healthy arriving in Kathmandu, and we fully intended on staying that way. This meant not drinking any tap water or drinks with ice and brushing teeth only with bottled water. No ice cream, salads, or milk either. The much-feared "Kathmandu belly" was to be avoided at all costs!

After a big and protein-laden meal, we retired to bed and tried to settle in to our new time zone. For me, that was exactly nine hours and forty-five minutes ahead of New York City.

The next morning at breakfast, Scott did a quick team check. People were feeling pretty good as he reaffirmed taking precautions with food and water and other habits that could cause sickness. We all nodded in agreement before he came back with one final check-in point.

"I take it everyone was careful in the shower this morning? Meaning no mouths open under the shower head?" Necks swung around as each of us replayed our shower moves in our minds—clearly this would take serious conscious training.

The next day was final gear-checking with the guides, who inspected our gear to make sure everything was in order, similar to a pilot and copilot's checklist procedure before takeoff—there would be no second takes on the mountain. What we needed we brought in; what was excess would be left behind. Climbing is a lot about gear personalization and familiarity. Missing key items, however small, or having boots or crampons (boot spikes) that didn't quite fit could be cata-strophic on the mountain, both for us as individuals and, as importantly, for our team. With this crucial check behind us, Scott proceeded to the Nepali Tourism Ministry to secure our climbing permits. Everest permits are tightly controlled and prized; with each permit costing more than ten thousand US dollars, they are a key source of revenue for Nepal.

At 4:00 a.m. my alarm sounded. With mouth tightly shut, I enjoyed my last hotel shower before we headed to the airport. It would be a life without luxury or amenities for the next two months. The domestic terminal was a dilapidated hangar that felt more like a warehouse. All the weighing machines at the check-in desks were massive old scales. It reminded me of jockeys getting weighed in before horse racing. They were having a power outage when we arrived, but none of the staff blinked an eye. Regular life in Kathmandu.

I asked what looked like an airline official in a peaked hat if our 6:30 a.m. flight was on time. He furrowed his brow, rubbed his chin, and pondered for a few seconds before beaming a smile, reaching his arm out and pirouetting it like a pretzel, and said, "Maybe on time, maybe this morning, maybe today." I broke into a smile and laughed hard inside—as much at myself as at his charming indifference. Clearly, this was not JFK airport, and my New York mindset was officially disarmed and made irrelevant.

In this part of the world, tall mountains create their own unique weather—reports have to be gathered as much from word on the ground as from any fancy satellite images. Low clouds, fog, or the wrong wind conditions can prove fatal when landing a light plane in a narrow landing strip perched on the side of a valley at altitude. We soon heard word of bad weather reports from the mountains. Our flight was delayed by a long seven hours.

Two hours into the delay, a Western climber remonstrated the same airport employee I had spoken to earlier. Red-faced, the climber wagged his finger, incredulous at the lack of certainty and specificity about our flight departure, desperately trying to "control" the situation. One of the things mountain climbing has taught me is the need to recognize acceptance. This is not about acceptance for surrender but rather about acceptance for reasons of pragmatism and energy efficiency—understanding the things I can control, influence, and change, and those that I cannot. This frustrated climber was burning an exceptional amount of his own energy for zero return—energy each of us has a finite amount of each day. Anger, uncontrolled, is the most corrosive of emotions. Worse, negative collateral energy was spreading around him like a fallout cloud among everyone standing nearby. He was emotionally unraveling in a low-stress environment, without having set one foot on the mountain. We all looked at one another, and no words needed to be said. It was a prescient reminder of just how important individual and team emotional strength would be. We were relieved he wasn't on our team.

When the flight was finally called, we were led through the gate and out onto the asphalt to a small ten-seater, twin-engine Otter propeller plane. This plane, with its faded paintwork and thick black stains around the propeller engine housing, had been on many journeys over many decades. A man pumped fuel through a worn hose into the plane's tank from a small and rusted manual pump fuel cart nearby. We climbed a set of rickety stairs to find the internal cabin wall was peeling away from the aircraft frame. One of the pilots assessed each of us up and down and told us where to sit. Taller, heavier folks were spaced between the front and back of the small cabin to balance the weight of the plane. We were told this was crucial to allow us to take off and to increase our chances of landing in one piece.

"We have only one chance to get this right!" the pilot explained wryly.

I took a deep breath, imagining the infamy of our plane going down before we had even reached the foothills of the Himalayan range. With the turn of the engine and a large puff of black smoke, the propellers came to life. The plane rattled and our ears were filled with a din.

This could be the most dangerous part of the expedition, I thought to myself naively.

CHAPTER 3
BREAKING THE CORD

OUR PLANE RATTLED and shook its way down the runway in Kathmandu. I took a deep breath and held my camera tightly.

Our destination, Lukla Airport, is the entry point for Nepal's highest peaks, including Everest, and is often listed as the most dangerous airport on the planet. Built in the 1960s through support from one of Everest's climbing pioneers, Edmund Hillary, the runway is only 500 meters long, with a 700-meter cliff at its tip and a granite rock wall at the other end. It has no radar, no navigation aids, unpredictable weather, frequent crosswinds, and no abort options. Those wanting to avoid the excitement can take a twelve-hour bus ride to Jiri, followed by a six-day hike to reach Lukla, or pay an exorbitant amount for a seat in a private helicopter with an equally turbulent ride.

We lifted above the city lowlands, weaving our way up into the Himalayas through tight mountain passes and valleys of lush green vegetation. Despite being a fifty-minute assault course of white-knuckle mountain-dodging, the flight felt uneventful. The noise of the engines drowned out everything, and we experienced only a little turbulence as we approached Lukla.

The pilot turned his head and shouted, "Landing in two minutes, pull your seat belts *tight*!"

I scanned around us for the airport but could see only the sides of the valley, a mix of jagged rocks interspersed with conifer trees close to our left wing. My heart raced. I could almost touch the pinecones. A climber in front of me began blessing herself, her rosary beads spilling off her hands.

Out of nowhere, a tiny, narrow strip of asphalt appeared, revealing a massive cliff at its tip. Suddenly we landed with a huge thud, and I stared at the granite wall rapidly approaching. The pilots pulled the control column back tightly, bringing us to a hard stop just meters from the wall.

When I stepped out of the plane I took a massive breath. It tasted sweet—no more fumes of the city, just the purest of mountain air. For the next ten days we would be slowly hiking along 65 kilometers (40 miles) of narrow mountain trails through the Khumbu region, where many of Nepal's most spectacular peaks are located. Surrounded by snowcapped peaks, we would ascend over 2,700 meters of elevation in the process of reaching Everest Base Camp at 5,400 meters (17,700 feet). The reason was clear: we needed to acclimatize.

Air is thinner at higher altitudes; in scientific terms, there are fewer oxygen molecules per volume of air. To compensate for the decrease in oxygen, one of the body's hormones, erythropoietin (EPO), triggers the production of additional red blood cells to aid oxygen delivery to the muscles. This process takes time. If we hitched a helicopter ride from Kathmandu to Base Camp, we would likely pass out as our bodies wouldn't be able to fulfill their need for oxygen. So we'd endure a steady hike through some of the most spectacular mountain scenery in the world to allow science to manifest.

Before we set off, we sorted our gear and sent along our heavier equipment and supplies on the backs of yaks to Base Camp. It would be a while until we would see it again. As we started along the trail, the change was stark. We left all asphalt behind and the trail became a winding path through rocks, sand, and gravel—surrounded by tall conifer trees, rhododendron forests, colorful butterflies, and birds. The noise of civilization was replaced by the sound of the afternoon breeze blowing through the pine needles above, surging water running through the steep valley gorge below us, and our own feet as they crunched on the gravel underfoot.

After a couple of hours, we arrived at a small settlement of maybe ten houses, built of bricks cut from granite and covered with tin roofs. In place of windows were wooden shutters on hinges. Only one of the houses had electricity, and with this, a small TV. People were gathered around inside watching a Bollywood movie, and neighbors leaned in through the open shutters. This house's TV was a community affair. In the sandy street, three young boys, about four or five years old, teased a puppy with a twig. The puppy was jumping and trying to reach it before they'd pull it up. They were laughing uncontrollably, like they'd just discovered their biggest excitement ever. The puppy was equally excited by all the attention.

I became nostalgic about my own childhood. I remembered days when I would go out to play in the morning and the only rule was to be back home either by dark or dinnertime, whichever came first. My younger brother, Paul, and

I, along with our dog, would live through our imaginations in the fields and woods around our Irish home.

In my experiences working with many leaders and executives, they find it hard to look back and relate to their own childhoods, to a time of not knowing and of relishing learning. They have curiosity, but it tends to be highly focused on solving or rationalizing something. I have also noticed that the following two questions usually elicit a long pause from those with children: "What have your kids taught you about yourself?" and "Who are you when you're with them?"

Coming out of the womb, we are launched into a massive learning curve. The panacea of childhood feeds this unbridled hunger until adulthood, when something else happens. We start to rationalize, summarize, and normalize our experiences, and we begin to entertain judgment around what we know as much as what we don't know. The latter loses importance over time. With age, we risk losing our openness to learn, and the ego replaces the space to be curious.

It was the opposite in the mountain valleys of Nepal, where adults and children—all generations—were living through shared curiosity mixed with an abundance of humor. Standing in this remote village in Nepal, watching this incredible moment of sheer joy and happiness that only children can exhibit to the fullest, felt like a wake-up call. How easy it is to forget that sense of wonder, that sense of being in the pure moment, as if nothing else exists, where time slows and you can just be. No judgment, no opinion, just wild curiosity and fun. I was beginning a new life in this sacred place—letting go, one step at a time.

We continued our hike and after three hours reached

the small village of Phakding as darkness arrived. Here we would eat and sleep at the first of our Sherpa teahouses on our trek to Base Camp. Teahouses are something akin to a very basic hostel: a main room with benches around a heating stove fueled by yak dung, sleeping rooms with plywood walls, and a bed made up of a few planks covered by a thin pad and a blanket. They don't have electricity, which means the only source of light was our headlamps. Taking a shower was a luxury and one that wasn't free. Typically, five to seven dollars got you a warm shower for a few minutes in an outside shed and, as with the toilets, you needed to bring all supplies with you (toilet paper, soap, shampoo, and so forth). Toilets were located somewhere in the corridor or in an outside shed and were usually pit latrines. No thrones of comfort, but definitely good training and acclimatization for what was ahead of us. Mountains are indeed humbling places.

We received our first lama blessing and yellow strings to go around our necks as well as a *Khata*—a white silk scarf to wish us good luck and a safe trip. The Sherpa people are one of the ethnic groups of Tibetan ancestry native to the most mountainous regions of Nepal and the Himalayas. They are experts on living in and respecting the mountains and have long served as guides and porters whose local expertise has been invaluable for visitors attempting climbs in Nepal. I've climbed in many regions around the world, but these people have by far had the greatest long-term impact on me. They exude humility and humor with physical and mental strength, in equal measure. In other expedition countries, international guides often want to lead the locals in a directive style, but here the Sherpa are the ones with the wisdom and experience. Our guides saw them as equals, which was reinforced daily as they discussed and shared together, reaching consensus on many decisions.

I enjoyed solid sleep and was awoken just before dawn. Experiencing the decidedly cool morning air, I felt my breathing was deeper and faster, and it took more effort to get the same amount of oxygen for my body's needs. It was my first palpable recognition of altitude.

After breakfast, we returned to the trail with a big spring in our step and the excitement of our first full day of hiking. The day was exhilarating and offered so much to take in. We passed numerous Buddhist stupas, mani stones, and prayer wheels along the trail. Perhaps most impressive was the stupa, a symbol of the Buddha, an enlightened mind and presence. The monument was said to represent the form of the seated Buddha, meditating and striving toward enlightenment; the spire represented enlightenment itself, the pinnacle of Buddhist achievement. A pair of massive eyes was painted on the stupa, penetrating into the deepest corners of your soul. There was no place to hide.

The Sherpa believe in numerous deities and demons who inhabit every mountain, cave, forest, and river, and who have souls. These have to be respected or appeased through ancient practices woven into the fabric of Buddhist ritual life. Many Himalayan mountains are considered sacred. The Sherpa call Mount Everest *Chomolungma* and respect it as the "Mother of the World." As we hiked deeper into the trail, the respect shown for this world around us was ever present.

Turning off judgment, for me, was like someone switching a screen from black-and-white to full 3D color. It allowed me to understand the Sherpa, their traditions and environment, and how they were all woven together. In doing so, it built respect and trust without the noise in my head. Above all, it took me back to who I was.

Along the way, we had to cross the impressive Dudh Kosi River—a huge and aggressive torrent of freezing glacial water crashing over rocks and boulders below us, fed by the melting glaciers from the peaks above. We crossed it and its tributaries by narrow suspension bridges—some made of wood and some of steel but all adorned by reams of colorful prayer flags blowing in the wind. The bridges swung and swayed as the noise of the spewing and foaming water below filled our ears. I felt a disconnect from my extraordinarily busy life back in New York as well as a sense of increased balance, respect, and simplicity.

Farther along the trail, as quiet returned, we heard birds singing and felt the soft warmth of the sun on our skins as it finally peered over the peaks surrounding us. Eventually the quiet was broken by the sounds of yak bells coming from the trail in front of us. The long-haired bovines are the work animals of these mountain regions. Related to bison and cattle, this ancient breed of large animals is well-suited to high altitudes as they have larger hearts and lungs than cattle do. They don't have functional sweat glands and can suffer heat exhaustion above 15°C (60°F), so they live high in the mountains all year. They provide food and drink for the community in the form of yak milk and cheese, and their dried dung patties are fed into the heating stoves at each lodge. This community is clearly ahead of its time in recycling and green living! The strict rule is to always stay on the inside path of the trail and give way to the animals—a number of hikers have fallen to their deaths on steep hiking trails as a result of collisions. Each yak has its own bell and chime, and the convoy created enchanting melodies as it meandered along the trails.

As we stopped for a welcome snack by a juniper forest and ate our prepared sandwiches, rumors and village gossip of Brad Pitt being on the mountain brought smiles to all. Chatter about the movie *Seven Years in Tibet* added to this evolving tale. As we continued, our pride in our steady pace and achievement for the morning was quashed as we watched a trail of Sherpa porters pass us. They were carrying huge loads on their backs. As they came closer, we saw all sorts of materials—complete wooden doors, partitions, large wooden crates, and sacks of grain, to name a few. In many cases, the items weighed close to their own body weight, loads of up to 80 kilos (175 pounds). They wore nothing more than sandals or sneakers on their feet. There were no roads in this region, and all supplies and building materials for housing and living had to be carried—either on the back of a yak or on a porter's head—all the way up to 5,000 meters (16,400 feet). For us, it was a Herculean feat. For the locals, it was an essential way to earn a living. As they passed, their backs arched, they still managed to smile warmly and greet us with "Namaste." It was a humbling moment I'll never forget.

We arrived at the Sagarmatha (Everest in Nepalese) National Park entrance, where our permits were inspected. It was still quite early in the season and there were not so many tourists on the trails, which made me feel lucky to be able to take in the environment. The last push of the hike involved a long, steep section where we gained a lot of elevation while navigating a trail strewn with rocks and some slippery and exposed drop-offs. My heart pumping fast, I was panting as the pace inevitably slowed. As the familiar feeling of thin air from past expeditions came back to me, I knew what to do. *Listen to your body and take it slow, Vivian!*

In midafternoon we arrived at the overwhelmingly beautiful town of Namche Bazaar at 3,440 meters—a serene sight of stone houses with tin roofs painted in different shades of blue, red, and green, built on steps carved out of the mountainside in an elegant horseshoe shape. As yaks were herded through the narrow stone streets, the juxtaposition of an array of internet cafés connected us to the outside world for the first time in a couple of days. A historic trading hub between Nepal and Tibet, Namche is the capital of the Khumbu region and a popular place for trekkers to gather and stay for a few days to acclimatize. Famous for its yak cheese and butter, it has a thriving daily market and retains its ancient culture and hospitality. We would stay at Namche for two nights to include a "rest" day to acclimatize.

The following morning we went on an acclimatization hike to the Everest View Hotel at 3,880 meters, where we had a spectacular view of Everest in the far distance. It had some high cloud around the top, which we were told was the jet stream. For most of the year, the summit is being buffeted constantly by this jet stream, averaging 120 kmh (75 mph) wind speeds. Everest is climbable only twice a year: spring (before the monsoon) and fall (after the monsoon). For around three to five days in May every year, the polar jet stream begins to shift slightly to the north. This causes the winds to abate briefly as the air pressure changes in advance of the building monsoon, which comes in from the Bay of Bengal, bringing huge storms and precipitation with it. The jet stream will still meander back and forth, and that weather window for climbing Everest can quickly close, but this is by far the most common and most accessible season. Nevertheless, nearly 10 percent of climbers die in their attempt to summit and return safely. Additionally, hundreds of climbers have returned with life-impacting injuries, including loss of fingers, toes, and other exposed body parts, many of them having to learn how to walk again.

I stared at this steep and imposing tower of rock, the tallest and one of the most dangerous mountains on earth, completely unclimbable with its current weather. It was surreal to think we would be attempting its summit face in just five weeks' time.

After returning to Namche Bazaar for the night, we departed early the next morning for the steep climb toward Tengboche. As we turned past the hill, the busy sounds of stone being cut were quickly replaced by those of yak bells and a soft breeze whistling through the juniper tree needles. Our pace increased once the climb section was over and the ground leveled off. The sky was a cloudless and deep blue, and Tengboche monastery perched on a hill in the far distance with a perfect and full view of Everest to the right. It was a breathtaking start and one of the most inspirational hikes on the trek to Base Camp. We passed many hand-painted mani stones along the path, carved or inscribed with the six-syllabled mantra of Avalokiteshvara, a form of prayer in Tibetan Buddhism. The awareness of spirituality around us and within us inspired a sense of inner accountability around cause and effect and reinstilled the importance of humility and openness.

We continued along the trail for a few hours before dropping downhill, where we lost much of the altitude gained in the past couple of days to cross the river on an old wooden bridge. But the altitude lost must be regained, and we rose up for a few strenuous hours—a common theme as we navigated natural obstacles.

Tengboche, located at 3,870 meters, is famous for its important monastery—the largest in the Khumbu region. Its birth was the result of a premonition by Lama Sangwa Dorje more than 350 years ago that a special monastery would be built in this sacred place. Patience and resilience clearly count in this region: In 1923, the fifth incarnation of Sangwa Dorje realized this dream and established the dramatic structure. It was destroyed by an earthquake in 1934 and again by a fire in 1989 and was rebuilt twice. Tenzing Norgay, the first man to reach the summit of Mount Everest together with Edmund Hillary, was born in the area and was once sent to Tengboche Monastery to be a monk. Today about sixty monks call it home.

It sits in full view of Everest and Ama Dablam—the two great peaks in the region. All traffic heading to Everest passes through the dusty and unpaved center of Tengboche. It's a great place to sit and watch the yaks, trekkers, and porters as they go about their business.

We found our teahouse where we finally rested and spent the night. The teahouse was very basic, with no electricity or running hot water. In the center of the room was the yak dung–fired stove, which was the only source of heat at night. We gathered on uncomfortable wooden benches and tables, absorbing the heat and flickering solar-powered lights, and ordered one token round of beers to soften the conditions. Drinking alcohol at this altitude is an experience in itself because a little goes a very long way. We regaled one another with stories, wit, and wisecracks from the day's hike and our past lives back on distant continents.

Our camaraderie was interrupted as the front door

swung open and out of the pitch-darkness two men helped carry a German trekker into the room. Her face was ashen in color and she was barely conscious. She mumbled that she wanted to continue the walk down the mountain. Clearly hallucinating, she was in no condition to stand, let alone walk. The two people with her looked exhausted and deeply concerned.

"Excuse me, is there is a doctor in the lodge?" they shouted above the chatter.

The large table beside us suddenly came to life in the dim light—it turned out it was a group of fifteen doctors on a research trip. Fitting her finger into a pulse oximeter, they discovered her oxygen saturation was 57 percent. Normally anything below 80 percent is a significant concern. In effect, she was suffering from acute pulmonary edema: her vital organs were under threat and death was likely to follow. They carried her to a room nearby and injected her with a powerful steroid. Fortunately, the medical team had a Gamow bag with them, a hyperbaric chamber pumped full of pressurized and oxygenated air to replicate a much lower altitude.

The doctors stayed up all night on a shift system to manually pump air into the bag. By morning, the woman had recovered somewhat to an oxygen level of 85 percent, and an evacuation helicopter was called to transport her to Kathmandu. It was a big wake-up call for all of us—to see how delicate the human body is, even at the lower altitude four days' hike below Base Camp.

We trekked onward to Deboche—a small and isolated village and its monastery, where we stopped for some time. Scott, our lead guide, told us we would need to be blessed here by the local lama and that this ceremony was very important to our Sherpa team. In simple terms, we would be unable to proceed farther until completing this. The Sherpa deeply respect the mountain and honor it accordingly. It was a sign of respect from us, and we saw their faces light up with comfort and pride in having us meet and be blessed by their lama.

We were ushered into a small and dimly lit room. On the far wall were dozens of photos of Everest climbers who had passed through this monastery. They had written thank-you notes on the pictures. The lama was sitting serenely on a bench in a corner. A man well into his seventies, he wore a thick red robe and held a distinct presence in the room. Our Sherpa guides introduced us, and when it was my turn, I sat cross-legged across from him. After writing a prayer on a card, he recited a chant while looking deeply into my eyes. His eyes were intense but kind. I could feel the presence of a wise man—someone who had nothing to prove. After the chant he pulled my head against his, our foreheads touching briefly before he put a Khata (blessed shawl) around my neck and then a string with a tiny, tightly folded paper prayer attached.

It felt as though he could see right into my soul. For a while, both during and after, I wondered what he saw. It was a moment of intense vulnerability and humility. I felt like an individual who still had so much to learn. It's interesting how life will give you these moments—sharing a connection with a complete stranger who speaks no English yet who can instill a memory so powerful. To be seen and understood is what we all crave.

As we left the monastery and came back into full light, I saw Bill sitting beside a wall, sweating profusely. He'd become incapacitated from a stomach bug. Our time in the teahouses caused unavoidable exposure to other hikers, and almost everyone had come down with some sort of bug or illness, including lung infections, fevers, colds, and diarrhea. Scott was suffering a lingering lung infection and a painful cough. Infections know no hierarchies or boundaries on mountains, and it was a reminder that we needed to be vigilant and listen to our bodies. Forever polite, Bill implored us to leave him there for a while and carry on.

"I need a bit of time to rehydrate and rest a bit here. I'll catch up with you guys."

We continued for a few more hours, arriving at Dingboche at 4,530 meters in the early afternoon, and Bill arrived soon after. We checked into a teahouse, Snow Lion Lodge, run by a magnanimous woman called Mingma, who became a mother to us for the next few nights. Mingma was a character; she ran her lodge for the spring and summer seasons and then traveled to France, where she was a cook for six months. She was like many of the local people we spoke with—hardworking, taking on multiple jobs to survive and make a living throughout the year.

We stayed at this altitude for two days to acclimatize, eating, chatting, playing cards, and stretching our legs without going too far. The aim was to acclimatize and make it easy for us to recover while also building fat reserves for the higher-altitude camps, where our bodies simply wouldn't be able to maintain weight and our stamina would be tested. We enjoyed the more relaxed environment of being so high on the trail with few trekkers. We were still quite early in Nepal's trekking season; most tourists went to Namche Bazaar before turning around to avoid mountain sickness and the colder early spring weather of higher villages.

The following morning we awoke to a snow-covered scene. It was just a dusting, but the entire valley landscape had been transformed. When I stepped outside, the snow crunched under my boots. I breathed in the crisp dawn air and committed myself to a day of doing my own stuff. We'd been together as a group for more than a week, and it was a rare chance to spend some time alone and reflect on what lay ahead.

After breakfast, the sun rose above the surrounding peaks and its flickers of warmth quickly melted and evaporated the snow. I grabbed my backpack and hiked up to an abandoned hermit monk's cave at 5,000 meters on the side of a steep hill. The location, combined with the advent of clouds and an increasingly blustery wind, exaggerated the feeling of remoteness. It was the first time I could enjoy the silence, which only an introvert can appreciate. I sat on some rocks and ate my lunch, watching a flock of ravens and yellow-billed choughs pass overhead. Members of the crow family, these clever and resourceful birds follow hikers up the trails and clean up any scraps of food left behind. They soar on the thermals with minimal effort, reaching great altitudes during the day, and return to lower villages and relatively milder temperatures in time for nightfall.

I grabbed my camera and captured the spirit of the place in a unique photo of crows and prayer flags wrestling in the wind against a moody sky. We were climbing higher, and the weather was feeling more extreme with each passing day. It still felt surreal that I was there—almost eighteen months of planning, and every step a statement of progress and momentum. I felt elated and anxious at the same time. I spent a couple of hours on that hill. Closing my eyes, I imagined I was back in Ireland—and I felt the same wild and fresh wind on my face. Memories and feelings for family filled my mind and soul.

I returned to the teahouse shortly before dark to find a ten-year-old boy proudly setting up the yak dung–fired stove for the night. It puffed and belched sweet-smelling black smoke as the dung ignited and he masterfully blew the embers. It was a family affair here, and kids were enthusiastically helping out with a whole range of chores. Mingma's cooking prowess and experience were showing through, and we feasted on a range of stews, soups, and Nepali rice dishes. My roommate, Ania, had also ventured out for a hike, but she forgot her water. She returned dehydrated and weak and ended up catching a cold as well as a minor chest infection overnight. Once again, the delicateness of the human body was plain to be seen as was the risk of any omission at this height.

After our customary hearty breakfast, we hit the trail, hiking along a relatively flat path as we cut through a dusty and windswept valley. On either side the mountains and peaks got taller and more jagged—their imposing shards of solid rock creating growing shadows across the landscape. It felt as though the Himalayas themselves were alive, possessing a sort of *Lord of the Rings* character, watching us carefully as we passed quietly under their supervision. In fact, I learned that the Himalayas are indeed alive—being a relatively young mountain range, they continue to rise from the earth's mantle, and Everest grows a full 5 centimeters (almost 2 inches) a year.

On the upper slopes we noticed scree (loose stones or rocky debris) and above this an odd light gray color, which turned out to be the remnants of a mountain glacier. A convoy of yaks passed us on the trail, their bodies laden with sacks of food, tents, and cookware. One of them was strapped with two large sacks of potatoes. My Irish taste buds watered as I imagined some spuds with Kerrygold butter melting in them at Base Camp. You can take a man out of Ireland, but you can never take Ireland out of the man. Coming from a small island in the North Atlantic, family and cultural ties were acutely felt and ever present. Even though I had emigrated twenty years before, Ireland was my rock and my family base.

We'd been on the trail for more than a week, and the hikes tended to be quiet affairs. Much of our small talk in getting to know one another had been covered, and people felt more comfortable being with their own thoughts for longer stretches of time. Our pace gradually got slower and more measured as we ascended higher and higher. The landscape continued to change with altitude; trees and bushes were replaced by more rock, gravel, and the occasional hardy ground plant.

That day's hike was about 5 kilometers (3 miles). It doesn't sound like much, but at that altitude it could take anywhere from five to six hours. After three hours, we began climbing a long and steep trail strewn with large boulders. In some places we needed to use our arms to help balance ourselves as we squeezed between rocks and navigated the obstacles. After an extended push, we came to the crest of a hill and reached a windy, bare, and exposed plateau, where human-made cairns (small stone monuments) and prayer flags were distributed over a sizable area.

As soon as the last of us arrived, Scott called us together. He asked us to huddle close in a circle with arms around one another's shoulders. He had a serious look on his face as he looked at each of us and spoke in a clear but soft tone.

"This is the Everest Memorial—a very sacred place for the two hundred-plus people who have died on the mountain. None of these people planned on not coming home. I want us to take a break and spend time here, each of you with your own thoughts about what this represents and about what we have ahead of us."

As I slowly walked around, the significance of this desperately lonely and piercingly somber place washed over me. A fog rolled in around us, enveloping the background. Each monument was different in some way and had the names of the climbers carved into the rock or on a rusted plate. These were built on behalf of the families of the climbers as a permanent memory to their soul and spirit. The signs were in an array of different languages, highlighting the fact that we may come from all corners of the world, but on a mountain we are one people, sharing the same risk.

One of the most striking tributes for me was Scott Fischer's memorial—one of the most experienced climbers in the world, he succumbed to the infamous storm of 1996, when eight people perished. It was a reality slap across our faces, and, for the first time, I genuinely felt fear about what I was embarking on. Sizing myself up to these mountaineering legends who, despite their experience, courage, and strength, lay frozen on the upper slopes of Everest, I felt undeserving, unprepared, and above all, alone. In this windswept place, it was inescapable.

After about thirty minutes, we continued up the trail and within an hour arrived at our final teahouse and last night's accommodation before Base Camp—the tiny village of Gorak Shep. Located at the base of the peak Kala Patthar, it had been the original Base Camp for Everest in the 1950s.

It was hard to sleep at almost 5,200 meters. I felt the pressure in my brain as a headache set in for the evening. When my alarm rang at 3:30 a.m., I got dressed, grabbed my small backpack, and left alone in the freezing darkness to hike up Kala Patthar, hoping to be in time to see the sunrise over Everest. Due to the structure of Everest, you can't see the summit from Base Camp, but this gave me a front-seat view. My headlamp lit the way as I hiked up the steep and dusty scree trail, listening to my own breath and the sound of my boots. After a couple of hours, I arrived at the summit ridge and ate an apple and guzzled some water while the horizon slowly began to illuminate.

The black gradually turned to blue as the sky became immersed with light. Eventually, the sun appeared over the mountainous horizon and flooded long tangerine-colored rays of light across the side of Everest, then over the ranges and valleys around me. It was a spectacular sight as all was revealed. With not a single piece of vegetation at this altitude, the only colors to be seen were orange, blue, black, and white. Everest was pristine, and the sheer scale was hard to take in. Sagarmatha—*"goddess of the sky"* in Nepalese—was revealed before me. At the summit there was what looked like a small white plume of cloud on its ridge. As the light expanded it became clear that it was an ice plume, highlighting the existence of violent jet stream winds at the summit, whipping up ice crystals and creating a dancing form. I savored the moment for a while before making my way down the hill at speed—elated at witnessing a new day being born in this unique setting.

After a ravenous breakfast, we left for the final hike—about three hours across very difficult terrain. We finally crossed the Khumbu glacier, climbing a small ridge on the other side to find a multitude of small orange dots in the far distance.

"Our first sight of Base Camp," I shouted. I gave Bill a high five and a hug.

PART 2
FACE-TO-FACE
WITH EVEREST

The might of Everest is palpable.

A gift from a
street child.

Bravery at Kathmandu: Just get on the plane.
Courtesy of Bill Allen.

Leaving the city far behind . . . nature beckons.
Courtesy of Paul Fejtek.

Kids and puppies—like my childhood used to be.
Courtesy of Paul Fejtek.

Namche Bazaar—carved out of the mountainside.

In the presence of wisdom. Getting blessed by the lama.
Courtesy of Ania Lichota.

Serenity meets
the peaks.

One of the many mani stones on the trek to Base Camp. Courtesy of Paul Fejtek.

The team left to right: Scott Woolums, me, Ania Lichota, Cindy Abbott, Bill Allen, Denise Fejtek, and Paul Fejtek.

Food supplies en route to Base Camp.
Courtesy of Scott Woolums.

Crows, wind, and prayer flags.

Pure inspiration: Everest sunrise from Kala Patthar.

Five-star living: our home at 5,400 meters (17,700 feet) for the next six weeks. Courtesy of Bill Allen.

Daily avalanches surround us and echo through the valley.
Courtesy of Paul Fejtek.

The real rock stars: our Sherpa climbing team. Courtesy of
Ania Lichota.

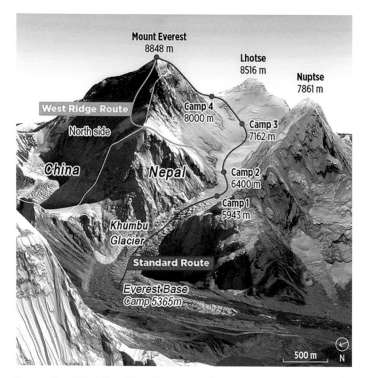

Source: Great Tibet Tour, https://www.greattibettour.com/tibet-travel-tips/
mount-everest-maps.html.

Everest route map.

Khumbu Icefall obstacle course: aka, snakes and ladders. Courtesy of Scott Woolums.

A fear like no other. Courtesy of Scott Woolums.

Legs shaking and mind racing . . .

Me heading into the abyss. It's impossible not to look down. Courtesy of Ania Lichota.

Don't trust all ladders—abseiling instead.
Courtesy of Paul Fejtek.

Base Camp boredom and reflections about legacy.

Team photo before ascending the Lhotse Face.
Courtesy of Scott Woolums.

CHAPTER 4

HOUSTON AT 5,400 METERS

FROM THE RIDGE we walked down into the glacial valley before us and made our way toward the signs of civilization in the distance. The path inward had us weaving through a mass of broken glacial moraine that included massive boulders, rocks, small lakes, and torn pieces of ice. On our right side, we passed the debris of a number of helicopters—their mangled bodies a stark and alien contrast to this extreme and remote environment of rock and ice, and a reminder of the invisible danger of altitude. They had crashed while ferrying and rescuing climbers who were either injured or unable to descend the mountain. There have been three helicopter crashes since 1997 near Base Camp alone. The thought of losing my life after believing I'd been rescued and on my way to safety was not a pleasant one.

After almost an hour we reached a large cairn covered by a mass of prayer flags and a weathered, hand-painted sign that read "Welcome to Everest Base Camp." Around the cairn were a few tents with people selling some food and hot drinks and a lot of people standing around taking pictures. I asked if we were stopping here, and Scott turned around and lowered his voice to little over a whisper.

"I'll let you know when we're stopping." In fact, this sign was a ruse to allow day trekkers to believe they had made it to Base Camp, hopefully deterring them from getting close to the climbing expedition tents, which were still quite a distance farther up the valley. The teams didn't want any additional risk of bugs or illnesses coming into camp and potentially infecting those preparing for the climb ahead.

Twenty minutes farther along the trail, we entered a small tent city where various climbing team expeditions had set up base camps. Spread over a sprawling area, it consisted of about 350 foreign climbers and the same number of Sherpa guides as well as support staff. It was a hive of activity and positive vibes as people settled into what would become their home for the next six weeks. In total, there were twenty-one climbing expedition teams on the Nepalese side of Everest, including our team, and we would be sharing the mountain with them.

Our expedition camp was located at the top end of the valley, close to the entrance to the Khumbu Icefall. It was a trade-off. We'd be living at a higher altitude, which, while good for acclimatization, would be tougher on our bodies. But we were also closer to the Icefall and thus less energy would be expended getting to and from this area as we began our training and rotations. In addition, we were separated from the busier part of the encampment, which would be safer for us in terms of limiting contact with other teams.

A white tarpaulin sign reading "Mountain Trip Everest Expedition" wrapped the side of the large orange-domed team tent. This would be where we would eat, plan, and hang out together over the weeks ahead. Inside was something akin to a Bedouin tent—a true home away from home. Along one side were plastic chairs and tables stacked with all kinds of snacks, condiments, and necessities. On the other side stood a long table that looked like a command center with a smorgasbord of electronic equipment, including two-way radios, satellite phones, a modem, laptops, batteries, and solar-powered lighting. Our version of Houston ground control.

Behind our team tent were our individual climber and guide tents, a line of seven of them. Mine was second from the end, just behind the "honeymoon tent" where Paul and Denise had taken up abode. I couldn't help thinking about how marriage and love could be tested at this altitude— definitely a case of survivor romance. I unzipped my tent to find my two large duffel bags that had been sent up on yaks ten days ago. I unpacked and organized my stuff until I heard the ring of a gong summoning us back to the main tent for lunch.

We were greeted by an impressive feast of mushroom soup, cheese, fries, and fruit—each dish introduced by our excellent and highly resourceful Sherpa cook, Surki. Fresh meat and fish were a true luxury as it was hard to keep food fresh without electricity, so we made do with Spam and canned meats for the most part. This meant supplementing our diets with other forms of protein and strength-building nutrients, including rice, eggs, lentils, quinoa, oatmeal, and potatoes. A highlight would be when the rescue helicopter brought up a few bags of fresh chicken meat.

After lunch, the entire Sherpa team assembled before us and introduced themselves. With beaming smiles, enthusiasm, and pervasive warmth, they represented a complement of twenty people in total. This included our team of climbing Sherpa, who would be with us on our summit attempt; the mountain support Sherpa, who would help with camp setup and oxygen transport on the mountain; and our Base Camp logistics Sherpa, who would keep us fed and supported. They were clearly as excited as we were to be part of the expedition. They were led by Dawa Sherpa, our Sirdar (head Sherpa).

The power situation at our camp was tenuous. We had kerosene for cooking, but all other power for lighting and electronics came from a large solar cell blanket draped over the roof of our main tent. On days with good sunshine, we had enough power to charge everything. On more overcast days, things had to be rationed. Mountain Trip had a server and a satellite modem, which we could all access daily for a limited amount of time. This allowed emails to be sent and received, although web surfing was painfully slow to nonexistent. Our location, in a valley surrounded by steep mountain peaks, meant satellites could be accessed only at certain times of the day, and it took a few days of trial and error to recognize the timing of our windows. I preferred to leave voicemails on my office phone, which could be uploaded onto my Everest blog by my assistant, Melissa. It felt like an easier way to share my words and experiences with family, friends, colleagues, and clients.

What was most interesting was the location of Base Camp. Surrounded by the towering peaks of Lhotse, Nuptse, Pumori, and Lho La, it was a rugged area with oversize boulders mixed with massive chunks of glacial ice. In the middle of the area flowed a small, vibrant river. It was a sight I'd never seen before—a shallow river of clear water flowing on top of the glacier through a channel cut into the ice, with a white bottom and white banks. As I peered into it, the realization hit: this valley was part of a live glacier. We were camping on something living and inherently dangerous, moving down the mountain at a rate of 20 centimeters a day. It was a bit like a Spielberg movie, when the character sits on a "tree trunk" without realizing it is the foot of a dinosaur.

After our long day, we headed to our tents to sleep around 9:00 p.m. The first night sleeping outside in a tent was a steep learning curve. With the bathrooms of the teahouses long gone, executive decisions needed to be made when nature called. If it was a pee call, I reached out for my pee bag (a reinforced plastic bag/pouch), sat up, kneeled, and carefully aimed into the funnel entrance to the bag. Being tired or bleary-eyed was not good at this time—sleeping bags don't like urine since the goose down absorbs liquids rapidly, is very slow to dry, and is impressive at holding pungent odors . . . so focus and aim were crucial! If one's bowels were calling, it meant a trip to our camp toilet—located outside, about 50 meters away through a path of rock and ice in pitch darkness and freezing cold. This consisted of a carefully chosen hole in the glacier located to one side of our camp, surrounded by a couple of rocks and covered by a mini-tent structure. It involved careful maneuvering and then squatting on a slippery/frozen rock to aim and release into the hole—no mean feat at 3:00 a.m. in temperatures of -15°C (5°F) with only a headlamp as light and the unal-luring aroma that only an open latrine could match to the extreme conditions. It would become a humbling daily expe-rience and acted as a strong reminder of the things I took for granted back in my normal city life.

At this altitude sleeping was difficult. Our tents were like walk-in freezers. My strategy was to strip down to my long underwear and thick socks, put on a sleeveless down vest, and then crawl into the sleeping bag. For the first five minutes, it was teeth-loosening cold, but ever so gradually my body heat started to circulate in the bag and it became warm. Typically, I would wake up after an hour feeling toasty-hot, strip off the socks and down vest, and resume sleep. My face was exposed, but wearing a woolen hat kept most of my head warm throughout the night. My growing beard also played its part in restricting heat loss. I had to do much more work to breathe, and despite full diaphragm breaths, I still felt short of air. After a while I dozed off, but I awakened after just an hour with heavy panting. It's as if my unconscious mind, which typically looks after so much of my bodily functions automatically, was ringing the alarm bells. My body was under stress and couldn't sustain itself properly. This impacted my sleeping patterns greatly, something I would fail to get used to during the entire expedition. It made for a broken night of sleep, culminating in one- to two-hour sleeping blocks, followed by being awake for maybe thirty to forty-five minutes before drifting off again.

At 1:00 a.m. a loud crack and sudden movement startled me from my deepest sleep. A grinding sound followed, as if something had snapped and was tearing itself apart. Then there were expletives and the buzz of tents being undone around me. I lurched forward, unzipped my tent vestibule, and stuck my head out. In the moonlight I could see three other heads, then a fourth—Scott's. He looked around for a second.

"Fun's over guys; it's just the glacier cracking under us. Get used to it; there'll be plenty more of this in the weeks ahead. We're pretty safe here." His words of reassurance didn't quite land, judging by the remaining craned necks, but true to form, he was right. The enormous weight of the glacier under us and its gravitational momentum as it moved down the valley created immense pressure, which, not dissimilar to an earthquake, had to be released. The cracking would become a regular feature at Base Camp, sometimes happening two or three times within a twenty-four-hour period. Eventually we would sleep soundly through it all and acclimatize ourselves to our new home at the bottom of the Icefall.

As I opened my eyes at dawn, they felt unusually heavy, and I had to squint for a few seconds. Grabbing a small mirror, I was shocked to see that all my exposed hair—eyelids, brows, beard, and head hair—was covered in a layer of white frost. I looked like the character in that movie, Benjamin Button. On the inside roof of my tent, the frost had formed a thick covering of crystals a few millimeters thick. As I shuffled around and the tent moved, the crystals broke off and fell as ice flakes, creating an interior snowstorm.

At 5,400 meters (17,700 feet), it got extremely cold—extremely quickly. I'd basically been sleeping overnight in a freezer, and the condensation from my breathing had frozen and turned to ice. Anything left exposed in the tent had frozen, including my water bottle, pee bottle, camera, sunscreen, and toothpaste. I'd have to wait for the sun to rise and the temperatures to increase before these items could be used. If this were a scheduled climbing day, it would have been a chaotic start, and one where I would be letting myself and my team down.

We were all highly driven, ambitious, and confident individuals in our own worlds and careers. Yet here that didn't count so much. We had to manage ourselves while being acutely aware of our impact on and our responsibility to the team. In a sense, we were like professional golfers, typically representing ourselves as independent, solo players, yet Everest was akin to the Ryder Cup, where the starting point of success was being part of something bigger and each team member was chosen to play their part.

The breakfast gong rang, and as I entered the tent I saw Scott passing around an oximeter to measure our blood-oxygen saturation levels. We would be testing ourselves daily and recording the levels so we could track trends. As witnessed earlier, having this level drop too low was a harbinger of problems with our bodies' reaction to altitude. Health problems could elevate rapidly from that point onward, and we had to be aware of asymptomatic conditions that may be lurking. As we ate, stories abounded about broken sleep—with many shades of excitement and anxiety around the realization that we were actually here, at Base Camp, the foot of Everest.

We ate all meals together as a team with no exceptions, unless we were physically unwell. The meals gave us a chance to spend scheduled time together while seeing and hearing one another and understanding our mannerisms, quirks, and preferences. Understanding the differences in our behavior in the Death Zone—altitudes above 8,000 meters (26,250 feet), where the amount of oxygen is insufficient to sustain life—would be a crucial part in judging risk and assessing options.

We learned to bond with one another, and we established routines, which invited and promoted sharing—not just about the climb but also to reveal our personalities and allow us to open up. Humor and laughter were key components of this. We could be serious, responsible, and highly focused while training on the ice, yet change gears and become irreverent, silly, fun, and deeply relaxed at night after dinner. It released us to be our true selves, and the energy created as a result of that genuine vulnerability was infectious. Hysterical laughter often ignited—jokes, snipes, witty comebacks, and wildly entertaining stories, some true and some ingeniously creative, lit up our spirits on a daily basis. This multidimensional, dynamic relationship is what allowed us to fully connect our minds and personalities—and it became our bedrock, both as a unified team and as individuals, throughout our Everest expedition. It would be used interchangeably with great effect in times of crises, focus, compassion, and humor. We were putting the framework and building blocks in place, and our leader, Scott, understood this clearly.

We spent the next few days in camp acclimatizing and falling into a routine. I felt like Bill Murray in *Groundhog Day*, each day waking to the same schedule of breakfast, lunch, and dinner with the team and the Sherpa. The weather made its daily cameo: bright sunshine and piercing blue skies in the morning, followed by a buildup of cumulus clouds around noon, and then a snowstorm for a few hours through late afternoon, leaving a blanket of maybe 10 centimeters (4 inches) of snow, which quickly froze as the sky cleared and the sun set.

Some days, as the sunbeams raised the temperature, some of the hardpacked snow—often encased in huge overhangs on the peaks high above us—would break off and tear down the steep mountainsides and gullies, forming aggressive avalanches. It was a longer and more disconcerting noise than the shifting glacier beneath us. As the avalanche picked up speed, the rapidly increasing mass of falling snow and ice would roar louder and louder.

Its decibels pinged and echoed off the surrounding mountains, creating a surround-sound cacophony of physical noise energy throughout the valley. Once the avalanche subsided, we would count ten to fifteen seconds and watch the fallout snow, a cloud of ice dust, quietly reach us. It was truly bizarre experiencing the last stage of this enormous release of energy.

The freezing nights made trips to and from our tents somewhat of an assault course over snow and ice, but one look upward and your breath was taken away—a universe of stars so bright you felt infinitely closer to them, an air so cold and pure your lungs felt cleansed with every breath, and all around you the silhouettes of enormous, towering peaks. In those moments I felt truly alive yet living on the edge of life itself.

Our time in Base Camp was not just spent acclimatizing before climbing Everest in one long summit attempt. The mountain is so high and treacherous that attempting to summit involves breaking it down into three distinct pieces, or "rotations," over an intense six-week period. In a sense, it consists of a massive assault course of natural obstacles, which need to be trained for, planned for, and ultimately—through effort, timing, and luck—overcome. This involves a combination of equipment planning and logistics as well as human body training and acclimatization. Like building a new airplane or launching a new product, we divided the process into design, test, and trial phases before finally launching the finished product. Breaking things down into smaller parts limits inefficiency or burnout, where we can feel overwhelmed. It's the planning part, which can have profound impact on our level of execution and ultimate success.

The breakdown is as follows:

- Rotation 1: Leaving Base Camp to ascend through Khumbu Icefall (perhaps the most dangerous part of the climb—more on this later) up to Camp 1, where we would stay overnight. Then we'd move up through the Western Cwm to Camp 2, where we would drop supplies and stay for multiple nights to acclimatize before returning back down through the Icefall to Base Camp. This would take five days.

- Rotation 2: We'd ascend the Khumbu Icefall, where we would continue straight to Camp 2 and spend a couple of nights before attempting to climb the infamous Lhotse Face, where we would spend a night at Camp 3—located about halfway up the ice wall. Overnighting again at Camp 2, we would descend to Base Camp for one night before descending a couple thousand meters into the Khumbu Valley to the village of Dingboche, where we stayed on our initial hike up. This would take nine to ten days.

- Rotation 3: Returning to Base Camp, we would then begin the waiting game for the weather window for our third rotation—also known as our summit bid. This would involve climbing through the Khumbu Icefall to Camp 2, before Camp 3, and then on to Camp 4—Everest's South Col, where we would be best placed to launch our summit bid, if weather conditions and health allowed. This would take one week.

Distilling the climb down into these rotations allowed us to focus on one piece at a time. At a human level, this is so important. Our brain can become overwhelmed with choices and decisions to make, often burdened by multiple variables. Keeping focused on a specific number of thoughts, building confidence, and pressure testing were invaluable. This strategy involved three crucial action points: (1) practice, (2) practice, and (3) practice. Perfecting key elements of training was not for the sake of perfectionism itself but rather to build muscle memory so that energy could be effectively managed—especially in times of stress later on. In each of these rotations there was inherent risk, yet by breaking it down into smaller pieces, we could plan more effectively and be better focused on each task. Additionally, we strengthened our bond as a team as together we participated in and drove achievement on each part.

Before leaving Base Camp and attempting our first rotation upward, climbers and Sherpa took part in the puja ceremony. A literal "rite of passage," the puja ceremony is performed to make contact with the divine Sagarmatha/ Mount Everest and to pray for a safe and successful expedition. In the minds of the Sherpa, no one may step on Everest's sacred slopes before this ceremony of blessings for safe passage has been completed. The date of our puja was decided by Dawa Sherpa, our head Sherpa, who also happened to be a real and enlightened Buddhist lama. Other teams often had to request a lama from one of the villages below and wait for their arrival. We were lucky to have two lamas within our Sherpa team.

Dawa's Buddhist notebook said the most suitable day would be April 21, several days later than Scott had envisaged, but it wasn't a topic for discussion. It was another point of reflection for us Westerners, who like to work on a clock, calendar, and schedule—the left side of the brain sees planning discipline as a rock of strength on which progress can be measured, while this buffeted against the "actual" world in which we operated, which was full of situational realities. The physical frailty of our bodies, unpredictable weather, and, now, local culture challenged our preferences and comfort zones. We were in the land of the Sherpa, and we deferred to their preferences on local custom, which were nonnegotiable.

Time is a living and moving event that we cannot control. To fully harness it, we have a choice to learn to accept it and live with it, or not. It's really about living with ourselves. Our birth signals the beginning of our demise. Not to be morbid about it, but once the countdown clock starts, it cannot be stopped. Whether it finishes at fifty or one hundred years, every living moment in between is an experience, a choice to be savored.

While awaiting the puja, we tried to make the best use of the time by doing some training hikes to nearby Kala Patthar, where we savored a full view of Everest once more. Close to Base Camp, we scouted around and found a glacier ice wall, which we made our training base for a couple of days. A massive outcrop of ice 8 meters high (26 feet) was chosen, where we were tasked with climbing up one side using only a rope with our ascender (a device that, when attached to a rope, allows the device to slide upward only) and our crampons (boot spikes). When we reached the top, we had to carefully move sideways and learn to clip and unclip our safety carabiner at anchor points before descending halfway down the ice wall and then clambering down onto an aluminum ladder, carefully using its steps to get to the bottom, wearing crampons. A Sherpa named Gomba stood above me. He looked a bit like a Nepalese version of Charles Bronson, with a chiseled jaw and high cheekbones. He was clearly a strong and experienced Sherpa and, most importantly, had good intuition. He and I would team up again as a pair for summit day. Gomba offered guidance in broken English from a distance while Scott watched carefully nearby. When mistakes were made or I was too slow making the moves, Scott barked comments and criticism, reinforcing the impact of my actions for me and, as importantly, for the rest of the team. In this respect he was somewhat old-school and mixed emotions with authority.

I bristled internally at his tone, murmuring to myself that I was doing my best and wanted to learn without the grief, yet I could see that the responsibility for us clearly lay on his shoulders. He wanted us to be acutely aware of everything we did and be able to solve puzzles and challenges in real time while also building muscle memory through repetition. Additionally, it allowed us to value feedback, listen carefully, and reinforce the level of openness and transparent communication needed between us. Here, the feedback was among the guides and us; later, this would expand to feedback between climbers. It was Everest–climbing boot camp, and we were exhausted after the morning on the wall, repeating the same moves time and time again until we got it right—and got it right consistently. This would be invaluable as we headed into the Khumbu Icefall in the days to follow.

In order to prepare for the puja, a chorten was built. It was amazing to see the work that went into building this stone altar on a glacial moraine as a small Sherpa team chose the size of rocks—large and small—that created this unique structure. The result was a solid and amazingly symmetrical rectangle altar of stone on which sat saucers of juniper and incense. For the puja day itself, there was a hive of activity in the camp—the Sherpa were genuinely excited about the ceremony, which honored and celebrated the mountain. The chorten was decorated with cakes and intricate yak-butter creations, which our cook, Surki, had made by hand overnight. We were asked to leave our climbing gear, including ice axes, crampons, helmets, and harnesses, at the base of one side of the chorten in order to be blessed.

The puja is a moving experience for anyone who has had the opportunity to be part of one. The five-hour ceremony started with the two lamas in robes facing the chorten holding prayer books in front of them while the rest of us sat behind them. It was a complex and detailed event but very moving and fascinating. Our climbing equipment was adorned and blessed with a touch of yak butter before the chanting started. The chants and prayers pierced the Nepalese morning air with a deep vibration and resonance that could move the most agnostic of hearts. Thousands of years of tradition and culture matched with a unique humility and mindfulness in this moment. The ceremony was mesmerizing to watch as it quietly invaded our souls.

Each climber was presented with a threaded necklace to keep them safe and it was tied around their neck by the lama. As the proceedings progressed, levity gradually replaced the prayers, and people took handfuls of flour and threw it three times into the air. Soon after, the Sherpa came around and rubbed flour on our cheeks—a blessing that we would live long lives and see one another again when we were old and gray. A reassuring thought! Toward the end, trays of food and drinks were passed around, and we were invited to take them in threes—the number three is very special and a distinct feature of Sherpa culture, representing the three pillars of Buddhism.

For medicinal purposes, I'm sure, drinks included small bottles of whiskey and mini cans of beer, and after no time, there was a Sherpa–climber party raging with roars of laughter, warmth, and beaming smiles. It was a huge release for all of us, celebrating the past three weeks in getting here and passing through this cultural gateway to the ascent itself. The final event was to raise a long flagpole from the center of the chorten, with lines of flags stretching out in all directions. Suddenly the sky was filled with blue, yellow, green, and red prayer flags, which soon caught the wind. Each fluttering flag released prayers and mantras into the air and spread the goodwill and compassion from the Sherpa around us.

Everest is a never-ending roller coaster of highs and lows. The day after our puja ceremony, we heard shouts and raised voices not far from our tents. A group of people gathered around a part of the glacier where the crevasse was open. They'd found an arm protruding from the ice. Sometime later they uncovered the rest of the body of a climber, perfectly preserved. People wondered who this could have been and how this body could end up here at Base Camp. Upon examination, it was discovered that this climber likely had a tragic accident in the Khumbu Icefall. Falling into a crevasse, he was unable to be rescued and died. His body, encased in the ice, slowly moved down the mountain. His clothing and personal belongings led the Sherpa to believe that this climber died in the 1960s and now, meters from us, the glacier had finally released his body.

It was an upsetting afternoon and evening. I couldn't stop thinking of a family, somewhere in the world, who would receive a call in the days thereafter, a call they wouldn't be prepared for, relaying that their loved one had been found—decades after the loss of a father, brother, son, cousin, or friend. I lost my younger brother in a car accident and will never forget that phone call while I was living in Munich. I was twenty-two years old and completely unprepared to process the information and the emotions that went with receiving that call.

My thoughts spun around this climber and what his dreams were, imagining the world he lived in, his aspirations, and the family who never saw him again. My focus finally turned to the risks I was about to face. There were no guarantees I'd avoid the same fate, and I thought of the impact on my own family.

It was a long and sleepless night alone in my tent. We had not yet stepped one foot outside the relative safety of Base Camp. The mountain and all its risks would become a reality from this point onward.

CHAPTER 5

ICEFALL ADVENTURES

DINNER BEGAN as it always had, with our team gathering in the main tent and chatting about the day. Scott was glued to his computer checking the weather before he closed his laptop and cleared his voice.

"Tomorrow morning, we will begin our first rotation in our ascent of Everest—a three-day trip. We'll be climbing through the Icefall to Camp 1, before continuing to Camp 2, and then returning to Base Camp. It will be a long day and a big test for us. It's no cakewalk—the Khumbu Icefall is the most dangerous part of the mountain, and we need to be safe and fast, in that order. Our training, planning, and teamwork come to life tomorrow morning, and I expect each of us to play our part." His words underlined our change in mindset—more serious, more focused, and more exposed.

Our goal was to make our way through the Icefall and reach Camp 1 by lunchtime, where we would stay one night. The following morning, we would pack up and depart, navigating our way through the crevasse fields of the Western Cwm and up to Camp 2, where we planned on staying four nights to further acclimatize. As well as our usual backpack, we would share carrying equipment and supplies for Camp 2, including food, cooking equipment, kerosene, and tents.

There was little afterdinner chat, and I was back in my tent by 8:30 p.m. The excitement and anxiety were already taking hold. On the one hand, I was so ready for this next chapter, to finally leave Base Camp, progress up the mountain, and embrace the journey I had planned in my head for so long. On the other hand, I was anxious about the many obstacles and unknowns to be faced and how my body would respond to the altitude and conditions. I laid out my gear and prepared for the morning, then spent the next three hours awake, tossing and turning in my sleeping bag. Having had a fear of heights my entire life, I knew tomorrow would be a deeply challenging day as I would have to face and overcome my fears, yet again, using the power of mind over body.

Of all the obstacles and dangers on Everest, the Icefall is by far the most infamous for fatalities and risk. A 16-kilometer (10-mile) river of ice, the Khumbu Glacier is the highest glacier in the world and one that moves with such speed that large crevasses open up without warning, especially when the ice is funneled down through steeper sections of the mountain. The section between Base Camp and Camp 1 is known as the Khumbu Icefall. Dropping almost 700 meters of altitude over a relatively short 4-kilometer (2.5-mile) distance, this huge glacier is in effect squeezed down through a narrow gully in the mountain. Picking up gravitational speed from its sheer weight and mass, it moves at more than one meter a day, more than five times the speed of the glacier at Base Camp. It's this dynamic of fast-moving sections encountering blockages of rock and buildups of ice that result in it carving deep crevasses, some as deep as fifty meters. The weight of the ice creates enormous pressure as the ice piles over itself and becomes extremely unstable. Huge blocks of ice the size of houses break free, collapse, and tumble through the Icefall intermittently.

Towering overhangs of heavy accumulated snow and ice (some up to nine meters) called seracs can break free and fall from above, often creating avalanches in the process. Should a climber be caught in an avalanche or collapse event in the Icefall, there's very little they could do to escape. It is virtually impossible to run away or even know which way to run in such a confined space.

Each year, a team of experienced and hardy Sherpa known as Ice Doctors prepare what is determined to be the safest route through the Icefall for the climbing parties and support teams. In the process, they install more than two hundred ladders across crevasses, cornices, and ice walls and set up a fixed-line rope for safety. This installation is merely the beginning of their work—with the constantly moving glacier, crevasses and ice structures are changing daily, and thus *every* ladder, fixed line, and ice screw needs to be checked and reinstalled on an ongoing basis.

When my alarm rang at 2:30 a.m., I sprang up in my tent, though with heavy eyes. It was very cold (-8°C/18°F inside the tent), and I quickly put on my down jacket before walking outside to the toilet tent. My stomach was upset, and I had some diarrhea, likely from the anxiety. Walking back, I could see Surki and his small team in the cooking tent preparing a carb-fest of porridge, toast, and fried eggs for the efforts ahead. Our cooking team was filled with true champions—always dependable and resourceful at any time and during all weather conditions.

I crawled back into my tent, dressed, thoughtfully

layering my clothes—it would be very cold to start with and could well be sweltering by the end as the reflective rays of sun on ice baked climbers within the windless Icefall. I guzzled down water, an essential task ahead of a climb, as I finished packing my backpack containing some of my heavier clothing sets as well as the food and water needed for future rotations and our summit bid. These would be buried at Camp 2 and uncovered later. Also included were cooking supplies, which we were collectively carrying up with us; in my case was a cooking pot and a tin of kerosene. It made for a heavy backpack, perhaps 18 kilograms (38 pounds).

The final thing to do was put on my all-important boots. Everest boots are highly specialized—they have to be multilayered for insulation yet strong enough to withstand the extreme conditions. The only problem was that I had left my boots in the vestibule of the tent overnight and they were frozen. Everest Base Camp is higher than the peaks of three of the seven summits, but I had experienced this before in Antarctica and it was a careless mistake. Putting on cold boots takes double the time, as the boot is rigid and hard to get your foot into. Unsurprisingly, a cold boot also meant cold feet within seconds. Luckily, now I could go to the main tent to warm up, but this would not exist higher up the mountain—there was always learning and self-improvement on a mountain!

We left camp at 4:00 a.m. and performed the essential Sherpa ritual of walking three times around the chorten (puja altar). After a small prayer and a chant from Dawa Sherpa, followed by a blessing with burning juniper twigs and each of us throwing rice into the air, we slowly walked out into the pitch-black darkness. Snaking our way upward, we climbed in absolute silence; the crunching of our heavy boots in the snow was the only sound to pierce the freezing air. My thoughts were about focus and the importance of finding my climbing rhythm while readying myself for the challenges ahead. Equally present in my mind was the knowledge that we would be passing through a veritable graveyard for dozens of climbers and Sherpa who were unsuccessful in running the gauntlet and who had perished in the same Icefall.

Like many things on Everest, leaving in darkness in such a treacherous landscape is a matter of risk trade-offs. While harder to see, the ice is at its coldest and thus more stable and less likely to move. After dawn, when the intense sunlight begins to heat the area, the melting ice acts like grease and the ice blocks become increasingly unstable. Crevasses tear open and gravity and pressure are released. The most dangerous time to be in the Icefall is mid- to late afternoon, when the resulting avalanches can be seen and heard from Base Camp. Our aim was to get through the Icefall in four hours by the time we did our third rotation and summit bid. Today was about how close we could get to this goal while remaining safe.

After a couple of hours, we started to ascend steeper sections and took a break to put on our crampons—a steel frame with spikes that are strapped to one's boots to act as a foot claw to help grip the ice, especially over the steeper sections. We then attached ourselves to the fixed-line rope and began the clip-in, clip-out routine upon reaching every ice screw/anchor point, located every 8 to 10 meters. A fixed line serves three functions: it is a safety rope that will arrest any fall, it gives a leverage point in hauling yourself upward with your arms while your crampons give traction with your feet, and it indicates direction—particularly valuable in a storm or poor light.

As the horizon brightened, we took stock of the harsh reality of the landscape around us. The darkness had acted as an anesthetic to the danger, and now it was being revealed in 3D, equally spectacular and frightening. I felt like a miniaturized character in a kid's movie, an ant in a massive bowl of popcorn. The ice towers, walls, and seracs were enormous and extended in every direction. The emerging dawn cast huge shadows across these amazing structures as we began to see the crevasses ahead of us.

When I saw our first horizontal ladder, I felt a rush of anxiety. It served as a bridge across a crevasse 3 meters wide that appeared to be the tear point of a huge, slanted section of ice. The blue ice near the lip quickly fell away into a dark and most sinister black color, reinforcing its depth. The far side was lower than the near side, and the crossing point consisted of three aluminum roof ladders tied together with twine and laid across at a slightly downward angle. On either side of the ladders was a single piece of thin rope, to be used for balance. Ania and Bill crossed and then it was my turn. They stood across the crevasse, watching carefully and offering encouragement. Bill held the side ropes taut for me, so they were easier to grip, while Ania softly coaxed me.

"You got this, Vivian. Remember to breathe—we've got a bunch more of these so find your rhythm."

I clipped my harness onto the fixed-line safety rope and felt the blood drain from my body as I reached the edge and bent down to lift the balance ropes on either side of the ladder, pulling them until they were taut. The trick was to land each boot on two rungs of the ladder during each step to stabilize my balance and avoid falling. The ladders were narrow, akin to walking on a wooden plank with holes cut out of it. With crampons on, there was no chance to move or slide your boot once you'd committed to a step—the aim had to be solid every time.

I reached out with my right boot. My foot was shaking. I committed to the step but made contact with only one rung. Luckily, the two front spikes of my boot crampon reached the second rung and I managed a tenuous hold. I jerked the ropes tight and felt my whole body wobble. I looked down through the ladder into the dark shadows of the crevasse itself. A stream of sweat broke free from my hat and poured down my forehead into my left eye, where it stung—my already dry eyes reacting to the salt. My mind raced with thoughts of falling into the crevasse.

"You've never been good at heights," my inner voice reminded me.

"This ladder looks impossible to balance on."

"Maybe your boots are not suitable for these rungs."

My legs shook. My breathing grew shallower and shallower. I had to arrest this emotional slide. I did not want this reality. I challenged it with competing thoughts.

"You've handled heights before. Just steady your head and do it!" But I still felt the fear sapping my energy away.

At a breaking point, I took a huge breath and suddenly thought of my younger brother, Paul, who had died tragically some years before. He was kind, courageous, and inspiring in the nineteen years he was with us. Seeing his face was like a switch that turned off all of the noise in my head, filled my lungs with air, and poured calmness throughout every part of my body. I felt my legs firm up and I stepped out with my left boot, landing on two rungs. I took another step, and then another. As I reached the halfway point, the ladder bowed under my weight. I just kept breathing—my intuition finally locked on to its purpose. When I got to the end and finally felt the snow and ice under my feet, terra firma, I had no time to reflect. Behind me Denise was next to cross, and I had to pivot my brain to supporting her by grabbing the ropes and passing words of calmness and reassurance.

There are times that standing still is not an option. On Everest, we learned that in an inhospitable place, we absolutely need to keep moving. We would all face numerous battles with what I call Negative Internal Dialogue (NID). One negative thought can ignite a fire of negative thoughts (a negative thread). In almost all cases, they serve no purpose other than increasing your stress level and pulling you down into a spiraling emotional state. In the process, your energy is hemorrhaging, leaving you feeling depleted and making it even harder to act. I had discovered just being aware of this hijack is liberating in that it opens the door for it to be challenged or addressed. That season, there were forty crevasses to cross, which, over three rotations, equated to 160 ladder crossings. We had made the decision to climb through the Icefall and we needed to execute speedily on that commitment to reduce the risks, constantly and efficiently moving forward. It would require not just physical but a great deal of mental strength and endurance.

As the sun rose, we went higher and deeper into the Icefall, and the obstacles became progressively more complicated. Like a giant game of snakes and ladders, it felt as if we were ascending two-thirds of the time and descending one-third of the time to navigate past massive towers and blocks of ice.

We had to abseil down one massive wall of ice and cross a narrow ice bridge over a deep crevasse with nothing to help our balance other than the safety rope itself. The rope gave a false sense of security, and there was a constant need to have your wits about you. At one section, the rope wrapped tightly halfway around a large serac, turned sharply, and led into a glacial pond—a potential death trap—before we realized that this was the old rope and a new one had superseded it leading in the opposite direction. The Ice Doctors did their best to reset, adjust, and replace the rope, but with the glacier in flux, it was equally up to us to be responsible and judge risk in real time.

The farther into the Icefall we got, the more we could hear the glacier creaking and groaning beneath us, punctuated by distant collapses as the ice continued its inexorable journey down the mountain. There was a palpable sense of unease felt among all the climbers we met—that we were passing through this place on borrowed time. We stared in awe at the Sherpa teams, who overtook us carrying over-size loads across the same ladders and obstacles, ferrying essential supplies up to higher camps.

As we neared the top of the Icefall, I turned a corner and saw Scott standing and staring up at a massive ice wall, perhaps 20 meters tall. He shook his head as he looked at the three ladders attached to get us to the top.

"Those ladders look screwed up, and I'm not comfortable using them," he said. Frustrated but calm, he chose the alternative route—an equally tricky narrow and ascending ledge off to the right side.

I was the first to go and slowly made my way across. The ledge was about the width of my boot toe—in other words, not wide at all. I steadied myself and breathed. As the ledge narrowed even more, I leaned my whole body against the ice, unable to see my feet. With one hand on the rope, I used the other to desperately find any semblance of a finger grip. It was full-on intuition climbing. When I finally reached the end of the ledge, I made a mini-leap over to a foothold. I stretched my arm up to the top of the Icefall, searching frantically with my fingers before finally finding a hold to grip. I hauled myself up and turned around. A spectacular vista of the entire Icefall opened up below me.

The rest of the team climbed up and we took a break in what was now blazing sunshine to strip down to our inner layers. As we ate and hydrated, we heard a loud rumble and then the unmistakable crashing sound of an ice collapse down to our left. Luckily, it was below and off the trail, but Scott was not happy.

"Today, we came through the Icefall without incident, but what we just heard is exactly why we shouldn't be here. We were far too slow and because of that we put ourselves and each other in danger. This is unacceptable, and we've got to do better next time." His tone was measured but resolute. The time was just before 11:00 a.m. and we had taken almost seven hours to get through the Icefall. For every additional minute we stayed in the Icefall, our chances of experiencing a dangerous movement or collapse increased exponentially. This was a team wake-up call.

Our goal was to be cognizant of doing something for the first time yet help one another as a team. However, it turned out that our natural inclination was to overthink all the new things we were doing, get lost in our own heads, and ultimately take much more time than was needed to ensure our safety. Scott wanted us to work together and solve challenges together, pooling experiences and best practices in real time.

Our default was to worry about ourselves as individuals. Despite successfully bonding up to that point, nature and nurture were hijacks not to be underestimated. Reading one another's emotional states and engaging with them openly and courageously were key factors in being smarter and more effective together. It was all about finding our voices to challenge the noise. Becoming a team would take conscious work effort and lots of mistakes along the way.

After our break, we continued into an enormous and relatively flat ice field interspersed with open crevasses. Above us were spectacular views of the peaks Nuptse and Lhotse, set against a backdrop of a breathtaking crystal-blue sky. From that point on, the widest crevasses had ladders installed—the rest were left open and involved an extended stretch or jump to cross them.

It took another hour to finally reach Camp 1, where the Sherpa had set up our tents. For all camps above Base Camp, we shared tents, and I collapsed into mine, quickly falling into a deep slumber. Camp 1 was quite exposed, and a stiff wind picked up in the evening and continued until morning, shaking the walls of our tent constantly. It made for a stormy first night, but it was welcome rest nonetheless. My two hours of broken sleep the night before meant I was completely exhausted.

I was awoken briefly by my new tentmate, Ania, who had similarly passed out within seconds. Ania and I were climbing friends from previous expeditions together, and sharing a tent brought familiarity and levity to a highly stressful environment. As a team, most of us were feeling the altitude, with lightheadedness and headaches. In addition, Ania was still recovering from a sickness she had picked up at Base Camp the week before and was on antibiotics. And

Cindy had a terrible cough throughout, which seemed to get worse with altitude.

The following day was an acclimatization day, which meant we would conserve our energy and allow our bodies to get used to the lower oxygen levels. This camp was temporary; we wouldn't be staying here during rotations 2 and 3 when we would climb directly from Base Camp to Camp 2. This meant there was no main tent, so we kept it simple by just boiling water and eating noodles or ramen in our own tents. The toilet situation was equally basic—with no facility on hand and honoring our code of Leave No Trace, we used green plastic wag bags and carefully sealed them, hoping they would stay frozen until we returned to Base Camp. Our priority was to remember where the bags were stored and make sure they didn't lie in the sun. Typically, an acclimatization day at the lower camps would involve some stretching of legs and a small hike, which we did after breakfast. It was important for our bodies to experience an increase in altitude, even if only for a few hours, before we returned to camp. The following day, we would leave for Camp 2 and break through the 6,000-meter (19,680-feet) altitude mark.

The next morning dawned with a blustery wind and very cold conditions. Packing up our supplies, we collapsed our tents and started the process of moving camps, leaving just one emergency tent buried in the snow. At 8:00 a.m. we began our long walk up to Camp 2 through a surreal valley called the Western Cwm. Named by George Mallory, an early pioneer of Everest, *cwm* is the Welsh word for a glaciated valley. Although it had the appearance of a broad, flat, and undulating valley and potentially a steady and uneventful climb, the reality was far different. The central section was torn open by massive lateral crevasses blocking a direct route. We had to turn off to the far right, to the base of Nuptse, where we entered a narrow and dangerous passage called Nuptse Corner. Climbing down into some of the deepest crevasses reminiscent of a mini–Grand Canyon, we again encountered ladders and exposed cracks in the glacier. When we surfaced, we looked up ahead and witnessed a stupendous view of Everest's upper slopes, including its distinctive black pyramid summit. The black is the exposed rock, so steep that snow and ice are unable to accumulate. One can feel the sheer might of this mountain.

Commonly called the "Valley of Silence," the Western Cwm had almost no wind at ground level, giving an incredibly eerie feeling. As we progressed, the sun rose higher in the sky and we started removing layers of our clothing. Enclosed by solid rock on three sides, the snow-laden slopes surrounding the Western Cwm reflected and amplified solar radiation to such an extent that by 10:00 a.m., this hyper-bright valley began to feel like a furnace. We took a break, and while we sipped our water, there was a loud roar from ahead of us. On the upper slopes of Lhotse, a small ice collapse quickly turned into an avalanche. Tearing down the steep sides of the mountain, we felt the vibration through the air and then, a minute later, a large cloud of fallout snow/ice crystals reached us and blocked the sun for a few minutes. The moment the sun was shielded, the temperature dropped rapidly, and we found ourselves reaching for our down jackets and gloves. Here, the temperature variation was one of the most dramatic on earth—going from more than 35°C to below freezing in minutes.

After three hours, Camp 2 appeared in the far distance. I sipped my last drops of water and regretted not having taken more with me. I took another break and lathered sunscreen over my freckled Irish face, knowing that filling my pores would only increase my sweating and dehydration. Looking up at the sky, I prayed for a puff of wind or a cloud to pass over the sun and create a cool respite, even if just for a few seconds, as if in the desert. Altitude had taken hold, and my legs felt like lead weights.

Forty minutes later, I was parched and experienced what could only be described as a *Lawrence of Arabia* moment. My mouth felt as if it were full of cotton balls, and my tongue was dry. The silence exaggerated the heavy thumps of my slow steps in the snow and the effort each one took. Suddenly, I saw one of our Sherpa coming toward us with a large flask. I wondered if I were hallucinating. He soon reached me and with a broad smile passed me a large plastic cup of orange-flavored water. I chugged it like it was a pint of cool Guinness and he burst into laughter. Without asking, he poured me another. As was so often the case on the mountain, the Sherpa were always there when you needed them.

The last 500 meters involved a walk through some scree to the left side of the valley. As with all camps, the location was strategically chosen both for safety and accessibility to the upper slopes. We pitched our tents at the upper end of Camp 2, closer to the Lhotse Face and along the Southwest Face of Everest, which was directly, but far, above us. There were another four or five climbing teams at Camp 2, so we weren't alone. We heard from a neighboring group about a climber from Kazakhstan who perished in an avalanche not far from our camp the previous season and whose body still remained there. On Everest, safety is relative and never guaranteed.

As camp arrivals go, my body told me this milestone was an achievement. The stress and effort of getting through the Icefall two days before; the long, hot slog today; and a heavy backpack and dehydration all took a toll, and my body was weak and aching. The conditions had been a big test for us, but we all made it, and now, at 6,400 meters (21,100 feet), we settled in to what would be the highest altitude most of us had ever slept in, including me.

Camp 2 was colder and windier, with less air. However, on a sunny day, it was spectacularly beautiful. Standing outside my tent, if I craned my neck to my left full tilt, I could see Everest's summit cone almost directly above us. Straight ahead, the Lhotse Face rose imposingly for almost 1,000 meters, its blue sheen highlighting its glasslike, icy surface and near-vertical slope. Off to my right, Nuptse's almost 7,900-meter peak was in full view. And below us, we had an aerial view of the Western Cwm, the entrance to the Icefall, and far below that the gray-colored glacial moraine of our Base Camp valley. It was as if I were looking through a virtual reality headset with a full 3D view of the Everest valley—that is, until I realized my breathing was more shallow and rapid. With only 45 percent of the oxygen at sea level, the air at that height was thin, and I found myself mildly hyperventilating during my first hours there. This abated after a few days as my red blood cells multiplied and my brain got used to the conditions without hitting the warning buttons.

After a brief but deep nap, I unpacked and organized my gear. We would stay here a cumulative eleven nights over the three rotations. The first rotation would be three nights. Taking this into account, I had the genius idea to carry up a small foldable net seat, which I'd bought in

Kathmandu. It turned out to be a complete lemon and next to useless. Having lugged it halfway up the highest mountain on earth, I tried every conceivable way to make it work, ably supported by a river of colorful Irish language about its design virtues and quality. Ania supported the seat from behind as I tried in vain to squeeze my backside in and balance. When it collapsed for the fifth time, we began laughing hysterically and continuously for a good fifteen minutes. It felt like the perfect release from the stresses of the day's efforts and provided lots of witty banter over dinner with the rest of the team.

The Sherpa had set up a smaller version of our Base Camp main tent. Although just big enough to seat us at a table, it became an important social anchor during our downtime. We came in to read a book, play cards, listen to music, or just hang out and chat. The temperature at that altitude dropped like a stone once the sun set, and we ended up wearing our full down suits during dinner. The temperature inside the tent was barely above the freezing point. Surki did his usual masterful cooking, albeit with a reduced spread. Before heading back to my tent, I grabbed a plastic bottle and filled it with boiling water—my sleeping bag heating system. It worked like a thermal treat; warming the bottom of the sleeping bag as I sealed myself in for the night.

The next day was a rest day, although our team meal schedule remained the same, and we were all expected to show up on time. After breakfast, I took a walk around camp. It was a bizarre place, with jagged rock formations and shallow caves beside a field of penitentes—formations of elongated shards of snow and ice, some up to 2 meters tall, pointing toward the sun like sunflowers. The Spanish name came from their resemblance to a crowd of people kneeling and doing penance. I hoped this wasn't a sign from the gods.

In the afternoon, we sat around and played cards in the main tent and wrote in our diaries or recorded blog posts. Paul and Denise were being tracked by the NBC affiliate back home in Los Angeles, and what a great story it was: California couple managing marriage and survival in the Death Zone. It was a story people wanted to know about!

An enemy of rest days was boredom and lethargy, which could impact the mind and spirit. Too much rest at this altitude was not helpful; the body was degrading, regardless of rest, so it was a matter of managing the loss as efficiently as possible. However, the mind also needed stimulation and to have purpose. In order to achieve this, we would get out for small rest-day hikes, which burned energy yet exercised the mind. Putting on equipment and leaving and returning as a team allowed us to find our pace and breathing rhythm while staying safe—a smart way to keep our focus sharp and our bonding tight.

On the third day at Camp 2, we took a short hike up to the base of the Lhotse Face and had lunch at the bottom. While eating my sandwiches and sipping water, I looked out at the expanse of snow, ice, and rock around us. Absorbing the bluest of skies, for some moments I couldn't believe I was here. Despite a childhood full of dreams in Ireland, I never imagined attempting Everest. I wondered what I'd have to face ahead and how this mountain would change me. I could feel in my bones that this would take me way out of my comfort zone.

The next morning we got up at 3:30 a.m. and packed up to return to Base Camp. Breakfast was a grab-and-go affair as we would have a full lunch upon arrival. The descent would be much faster than the ascent, mostly a function of gravity and lighter loads since we had carried up some supplies. Just after 4:00 a.m., we were standing outside ready to leave when we realized that Paul and Denise were not there. They had slept past their alarm and bolted out of the tent looking shocked and delirious upon being awakened. I felt sorry for them; it was a super stressful start to their day as they jumped around gathering equipment and quickly packing, aware they were keeping the team waiting—a cardinal sin in Scott's rule book. It was a lesson for us too—none of us had noticed their absence until we were about to leave. Having respect and comfort between one another didn't mean we were infallible and didn't need one another's help. It started with awareness, and it was a collective failure.

We left camp at 4:30 a.m. and headed back to Base Camp in one push, without stopping at Camp 1. The Icefall danger remained omnipresent in our minds and our goal was to get through it by 10:00 a.m., before the avalanche drama started up. We built up a strong pace, and the confidence from our acclimatization days, combined with our bodies' feeling that every step down was a step into more oxygen-rich air, meant that we made solid progress. It was still exhausting due to the level of deep and consistent concentration needed to navigate through the Icefall and the infamous ladders, but we reached Base Camp by 9:45 a.m., which was a fast time. Scott was pleased.

Base Camp felt like civilization amid the sea of humanity around us—a big change from our exposed existence above. I peeled off my boots and saw that my feet—with blisters bubbling—were not happy. The sun felt warm and I sat on a rock and bathed them in the glacial stream nearby before drying them carefully. We enjoyed a carb-loaded lunch with eggs and pancakes, and everyone headed back to their tents to crash after a short night and a long morning. I woke up after two hours and it took me a few minutes to realize where I was—yes, that kind of deep, solid sleep.

Maintaining hygiene on Everest was difficult even at Base Camp, and I really missed being clean. There were no rental shower facilities available as we had in the teahouses on the hike in. However, while we were away our resourceful Sherpa had rigged up a tiny standing tent with a red bucket and the head of a garden watering can attached to a hole in the bucket, creating a pseudo shower. I was the first to try it, and it actually worked quite well. The water supply lasted about two minutes and was gravity powered, so it was more of a dribble, but heck, I could finally get clean after almost three weeks of wet-wipe body cleaning. I applied a spray from a mini-can of Axe deodorant I had with me and changed into a fresh set of underwear and clothes. Pure heaven—I felt reborn. I returned to the team tent and people started commenting on the odor and asked me to walk past them repeatedly—"Vivian, I need a whiff of clean!"

Our plan was to rest and recharge here for a few days before beginning our second rotation. It felt more serious in camp now, a buildup of expectation and focus in everything we did. Time was closing in around us.

The exhumation of the corpse at Base Camp the week before, navigating the Icefall, and facing the edge of death numerous times had formed a heaviness around one aspect of my life that I have never really given any thought to: legacy. The realization that if something happened to me here, on this mountain, and I didn't return, how I lived my life up to this point would be how people would remember me. The die was already cast.

So the next questions were: How would they remember me? Had I lived my life to ensure a good enough answer to this question? My immediate answer honed into what I'd achieved and all the things I had "done" in my life before this trip. Leaving Ireland, living and working in six countries, a fast-growth career, business school, starting my own business, climbing the seven summits—the list was long. However, the more I rattled off the achievements and chapters in my head, the emptier this felt.

Then I had a moment of clarity—would they remember me for how I made them feel? Would they genuinely feel better about themselves because of me? In all my busyness and achievement, I didn't think I had ever thought of these. The more it came to the fore in my consciousness, the more I thought of things that actually mattered: to be present, really present, with people and match my drive with equal amounts of empathy and compassion—to be less caught up with the race and enjoy the journey far more, together with people. When we remember someone who has made us feel better, stronger, more alive, we remember that person's spirit and we take that inside ourselves. This is legacy.

There I was, 10,000 kilometers (6,200 miles) from home, and I felt there were many things I would have wanted to say to people who had helped me, been patient with me, and been profoundly important to me in my life. I grew up in a house and indeed, country where emotions were not readily expressed, and appreciation was implied and understated. Sitting in my tent, I felt a deep disconnect with this and my past. I steeled myself and imprinted a commitment in my head that, should I make it down safely, I would change this and find my voice.

CHAPTER 6

ENDURING THE STORM

THE BOOK HAD BEEN staring back at me for weeks, and I did my best to avoid its gaze. Sitting on the table with the satellite phone and Scott's laptop, someone had left a copy of *Into Thin Air* by Jon Krakauer—highlighting the infamous 1996 expedition and the drama that unfolded on Everest that season. As a twenty-five-year-old, I vividly remember reading an article about the tragedy in *TIME* magazine while on a flight from Johannesburg to Nairobi. It was equally gripping and shocking. Sitting beside my boss, we swapped the article between us and imagined how terrifying it must have been to be there. Like many people, what was most gripping was the human decision-making that contributed to the event, and we imagined putting ourselves in their boots. Fourteen years later, here I was—totally unbeknownst to my younger self—approaching a similar goal and inherent danger.

After my come-to-Jesus moment about legacy, I had an urge to get real about the risks as much as I could before my summit bid. I finally felt ready to grab the book and turn to the first page. It was an intense read for the rest of the afternoon. The book was every bit as absorbing as the short article

I had read in *TIME*, although Krakauer's account was even more compelling coming from the words of a climber who had been there to witness it all. I absorbed the drama and anxiety, and I felt ready to take in its teachings and takeaways. Even though I would be climbing as part of an expedition under two seasoned guides and our Sherpa team, it was clear it would be up to me to listen to what my body was telling me and make the right decisions when those times came.

There was one line that stood out that I read multiple times to try to understand: "But at times I wondered if I had not come a long way only to find that what I really sought was something I had left behind." The words were powerful, although the meaning was not fully clear to me at that moment.

Earlier the same evening, Scott and Bill gathered us in the main tent and walked us through the oxygen situation above Camp 3. Scott unpacked a box of Russian-made "Poisk" oxygen masks, which looked more like museum pieces from World War II.

"This is my favorite mask. It's ugly and not particularly modern, but in my experience it's the most reliable of any mask used on this mountain," Scott announced. Ordered directly through his contact in Russia, these masks were hand-stitched, pretty flimsy, and no two were exactly the same, which was somewhat unsettling. We tried them on to make sure they fit our individual faces. Amid the smiles and laughs about our alien transformation, under the surface the realization was clear that these Soviet-era masks would be one of the most crucial pieces of equipment keeping us alive in the Death Zone.

After dinner, Scott explained our goals for the second rotation—the big-ticket event would ultimately involve making it safely to Camp 3, halfway up the treacherous Lhotse Face. This time, Scott expected us to be significantly faster through the Icefall before going directly to Camp 2, where we would spend five nights, effectively becoming our midmountain base.

That afternoon, I borrowed the satellite phone, stood outside, and called my parents and family back in Ireland. They had been tracking me avidly, and I could only imagine what they were going through. A woman of great warmth and resolve from the west coast of Ireland, my mother had initially tried to dissuade me from my summit attempts, but when she realized I was serious about it, she became one of my biggest supporters. My father was a rock throughout—with an intense and incredibly driven personality, the mountains and hiking had been a passion of his since he was a teenager. I briefly gave updates on the expedition and then listened to their supportive voices as they shared news of spring in Dublin, their garden, the neighbors, the Machiavellian Irish weather, and highlights about my brothers' families and children. The news and gossip lifted my spirits and I felt connected to my roots.

The alarm buzzed at 2:30 a.m., and within an hour we were leaving Base Camp heading toward the Icefall. It was May 1—now some two to three weeks away from our estimated summit date. Even though it was just four days after our return from rotation 1, the Icefall had deteriorated and there had been big collapses the day before, crushing some ladders and reshaping crevasses. Our path had to be rerouted by the Ice Doctors and looked completely different; there were now steeper sections to climb and navigate around. However, we were much more efficient this time, and we successfully got through the Icefall nearly two hours faster than our first attempt.

At Camp 1, we took a short break and ate some food and snacks before embarking on the long and hot slog through the Western Cwm again toward Camp 2. The heat was intense, and all the efficient progress and speed we made through the Icefall became a distant memory as the sun's radiation and lack of wind took a toll. At one point, I looked ahead and saw Camp 2 appear like a mirage through the heat haze; I joked to myself whether I was actually moving forward at all or if the glacier was moving faster than I was! As we arrived at camp, the clouds started building and the wind picked up. We could feel bad weather moving in, and we spent time carefully securing the tents. One golden rule applied: no crampons or ice axes in or near the tents. Any resulting damage from a misplaced boot could put our lives at risk on the mountain—a punctured tent could be quickly torn apart by the wind during a storm.

I had my own tent this time since Ania was recovering from her stomach illness and we wanted to limit any potential bug spread.

The conditions deteriorated rapidly, and by 10:00 p.m. we were in the middle of a raging storm. My tent shook violently as the wind howled through the valley. Inside, the temperature plummeted and every tiny gap between the zippers and the material became a wind vent for icy air to flood in. Sleeping was difficult as the intense gusts rattled the structure. At 1:00 a.m. I was so concerned that I got up, dressed myself, put my boots on, and crawled out into the darkness on my hands and knees to inspect the tent mooring pegs and supports by the light of my headlamp. Through the swirling snow, I could barely see the tent material being yanked and jerked and the massive stress and pressure the pegs were under. Memories from my infamous trip to Aconcagua flooded back to me. We had lost tents and equipment in a similarly aggressive storm at high camp there.

The heavy snow continued relentlessly. I carried some rocks from nearby to bolster the tent supports and built a mini wall to protect the back side of the tent, which was the most exposed. After twenty minutes of exertion at this altitude and temperature, I came back inside exhausted, freezing, and out of breath. I kept my gloves on and spent time reorganizing and packing all my stuff into bags in the event that one of the support poles snapped or the material tore, after which the tent would quickly break apart. If this happened, I'd need to get out fast and save my equipment from blowing off the mountain while avoiding frostbite, and then hopefully squeeze into another team member's tent. All of this would happen within minutes in darkness.

Climbing into my sleeping bag with all my clothes on, I rubbed my arms and legs vigorously for fifteen minutes to return the blood flow and, with it, some warmth to my body. I soon passed out and awoke a few hours later just as dawn broke. There was no abeyance from the wind. I made it over to the team tent and we had breakfast together—most of us bleary-eyed and sleep-deprived. Despite our situation, we felt lucky since we had planned to stay at Camp 2 for five days, and thus the storm wasn't impacting our schedule.

The storm persisted for almost three days with a power like no other I'd experienced. It was exhausting. Even though I quickly and logically accepted that I was in the middle of a storm and there was not much I could do about it, other than hunker down and wait it out, it was a grinding experience. The relentless violent bursts of energy as the wind blasted the tent built up stress in my psyche. It was as if my conscious brain accepted where I was, but it was still registering danger subconsciously and couldn't let go of it. The minutes, hours, and days went by painfully slowly. There was so little to do apart from eat, doze, read, and write in my diary. I had carried up Ernest Shackleton's *Endurance* about his infamous expedition in Antarctica, and it resonated well for the conditions!

On the morning of the third day, I had to dig myself out by clearing 20 centimeters (8 inches) of fresh snow that was piled up against the tent vestibule before I was able to stand up outside to stretch my legs. At camp, the storm was abating; however, it was still raging above us. I craned my neck to study Everest's summit wall, the swirling white plumes of ice crystals and snow buffeting the exposed rock and menacing black clouds enveloping the summit. It was like looking straight up into a tornado stack. The noise was incredibly unnerving—an echoing wail like a freight train in a tunnel. There was no ebb and flow, just constant howling with a consistency and depth I had never experienced. And then it clicked—this was the jet stream buffeting the upper atmosphere. In the way stood the exposed rock of Everest. Awed, I tried to take it all in. I had never experienced such a sheer force of nature. That this jet stream was the default weather on the summit slopes of Everest for almost the whole year was hard to process.

Later that afternoon, we took a hike around camp and surveyed the impact of the storm. Another team had some of their tents destroyed, and they were busy surveying the damage and recovering debris. We were lucky—we had some broken mooring pegs and one destroyed toilet tent, its poles snapped like chopsticks and material fluttering on the ground, but all would be recoverable.

The following day we got up early and left camp at 5:00 a.m. for our attempt to reach Camp 3, heading up the glacier toward the Lhotse Face. The conditions were as perfect as they could be there: a brilliant blue sky and crystal-clear visibility, without even a whisper of wind. The change in weather was bizarre. We stopped briefly for water and snacks at the bottom and agreed who would go first and who would pick up the rear. I stared up at what looked like a double black diamond ski slope (which is for experienced skiers only), only there was no snow—just blue ice glistening and shimmering in the sunlight.

There would be some difficult sections ahead, and we would stay closely together as a group to allow us to communicate up and down the line and help one another when the times came. The base section of the face was particularly tricky, with 75- to 80-degree pitches, which had to be climbed using every limb to grab, hold, and balance. We needed to carefully coordinate our boot placements so as not to catch the face of a fellow team member with a spike of a crampon, and we worked to find a rhythm where we could move up in unison.

My crampons became life preservers, each boot placement crucial to securing a hold. It was a relentless climb; one chimneylike pitch after another for forty-five exhausting minutes. There was no place to take a break, so we continued upward, one boot and one breath at a time. Above the base section, we had visibility all the way up to Camp 3 and it was a fantastic sight—a line of climbers and Sherpa hanging almost vertically onto a single rope, going through the well-trained program of clip-in, clip-out at the anchor points. It looked like they were climbing the exterior of a skyscraper made of ice.

After more than five strenuous hours, we arrived at an area the Sherpa said would likely become our Camp 3 during our third and final rotation/summit bid. Sitting in a recessed ledge, we ate lunch and surveyed the view with wonder. At 7,300 meters, we were on the cusp of the Death Zone, and I was now higher than I had ever climbed in my life. Eating was difficult here as one has to breathe at the same time, and even when I filled my lungs to capacity, the physics couldn't be overcome. The air had just over 40 percent of the oxygen at sea level, and it took focused concentration to find a rhythm to be able to breathe and chew at the same time.

Coming down the Lhotse Face was akin to a cat trying to climb down the trunk of a tree—never easy. Due to its steepness, we had to control the speed of our descent. If we were to slip or lose our footing, we would tumble down the line to the next anchor point in the ice. Anchor points are in effect temporary ice screws, and our body weight would be exponentially increased by the velocity of our fall. The impact of a fall would be an extremely violent pull on the anchor. Word on the mountain was there were absolutely no guarantees that anchors would hold if the pressure was too great. The anchors could pop like rivets, resulting in an unstoppable plummet down the glasslike surface of the Lhotse Face to a dramatic and fatal ending.

There were two ways to descend. I could rappel down backward, which involved coordination with fellow team members, using them as my eyes. Alternatively, I could make my way down the mountain headfirst, using my arm as a wrist wrap by wrapping the rope around my arm and using it in conjunction with my crampons. This approach was not practical on the 75-degree pitches but would work on the 45- and 50-degree sections. It allowed better visibility looking forward and was a significantly faster way to move as a team. That said, facedown the Lhotse Face in a Batman-like pose, defying gravity, brought back my intense fear of heights. So we ended up mixing and matching the approaches depending on the level of steepness.

I stared down the long line of rope, thinking about how every step mattered and error couldn't be countenanced. My thighs burned. I tasted salt as sweat drained over my lips. Each step involved most of my body weight sliding down to the front of my boots, putting enormous pressure on my boots, ankles, and crampons. My toes scrunched against the insides of the boot tips. There were about 30 to 40 meters of rope between anchor points, and each one had to be negotiated by clipping in and out with the safety rope. I took these points as mini rest periods for my legs as my brain took over, ensuring a careful and safe transition at the anchors.

We finally made it down to Camp 2 by 3:00 p.m. I hobbled into my tent, where I promptly removed my boots and socks. The resulting steam (from removing my boots) cleared to reveal an ugly sight—a plethora of blisters and one very red big toe on my right foot. From the looks of it, I knew the nail was dead, would turn black in a few days, and ultimately fall off. Totally wiped out, I fell asleep immediately.

Two hours later, I woke up with a raging thirst and a fever. I downed a liter of water and ate some snacks but didn't feel much better. As the afternoon wore on, I realized

I wasn't getting any better. A runny nose and a dry throat added to my ailment list, and I soon realized I probably had a cold. Eventually, I summoned the energy to sit up and change out of my clothes. Feeling as I did, I took a bit more care looking at my aching body and was shocked at what I saw. I had lost a lot of weight. Inspecting myself with a handheld mirror, I could count each of my ribs. All the muscle I had proudly built up ahead of my trip had disappeared. My body looked withered.

I had seen signs of this, but I hadn't registered their significance. At this altitude you had to be careful about appetite management and ensure you get the required caloric intake. Under the stress of this altitude, the human body, recognizing the oxygen deficit, begins shunting food through one's digestive system without that system being able to absorb it fully. It makes sense when you think about it—the process of digestion needs a lot of energy, so it's easier for the body to redirect energy to keep the essential organs (heart and lungs) functioning and to keep a person alive. Ideally, we needed to be eating 5,000 calories a day at Base Camp and trying to get as many calories as this as we ascended. But as we spent extended periods of time at high altitudes, the deficit was unavoidable. We were lucky if we ate 2,000 to 3,000 calories above Base Camp and perhaps 1,000 to 2,000 above Camp 4.

A tell-tale sign that your body is consuming muscle and its own reserves in order to survive is that urine becomes cloudy. I had noticed this over the past couple of weeks. Now I had reached a threshold where my immune system was impacted, hence feeling cold, but also where my fatigue was much more evident every day. The physical stresses of being on Everest, combined with the mental stress of so much alone time in a tent, were impacting my normally happy and upbeat state of being. I had to work harder to be positive, and it took more energy to maintain consistent concentration.

Similar to the legacy moments I'd experienced a few days earlier at Base Camp, boredom had opened up a can of worms facing a reality I had ignored or had been blindly unaware of. We are given but one body in this life. Through good and bad, ups and downs, there's no trade-in possible. It's ours, yet we don't own it or control it. We are just custodians. Being honest with yourself means also listening to your body and taking care of it.

I'd arrived on the mountain thinking my mind was the driver and my body was simply the workhorse. Getting the body fit was my sole directive; thereafter, the brain would take over and direct it toward success, hopefully. The Eureka! moment was when I realized that afternoon in the tent that my mind was out of sync with my body and the latter was giving up on me. I was internally disconnected and didn't recognize myself. There I was, on the cusp of entering the Death Zone, and I had taken so much for granted. I was ashamed of what I had allowed to happen. I've found this to be a major issue in the workplace, too, where at the leadership level, clarity, transparency, and effective decision-making are expected. Being overwhelmed and physically weakened can quickly spiral. Everest magnifies everything that is not in balance—things that are too easy to ignore in everyday life.

At dinner I brought up this topic and it became a big discussion point for everyone. Even our team leads, Scott and Bill, admitted they had found themselves going through tougher periods when they had to dig deeper to get through the day and when even small setbacks drained their motivation.

The following morning we made the trip back down to Base Camp. The weather was changing again, and it began snowing as we approached the Icefall. However, this time the air was humid with little wind, and the snowflakes were large, thick, and heavy. It felt as if we were getting closer and closer to the monsoon period, when the warming daytime temperatures combined with the increase in clouds and humidity are harbingers of things to come.

The descent was efficient and drama-free, and we arrived before noon. As I entered my tent, I saw that it was leaning to one side and the floor was completely lopsided. It took me a few seconds to realize what had happened. The living glacier upon which we were camped was inexorably moving down the mountain—and with it, our tents! Being away for over five days, the incremental changes were cumulative and noticeable. The Sherpa were quick to rebuild the bases and tent supports, so we once again had a semblance of a home after a few hours.

That evening, as a team, we reviewed our experiences and learnings from the rotation. The storm had taken a toll, both physically from being pinned down in our tents, unable to move much, and psychologically from not being able to bond as freely. With ailments increasing and a gradual wearing down of our bodies, we needed to take stock and recharge. One comment we all agreed on was that our climbing rhythm was becoming solid. Similar to members of the Special Forces, who spend extended periods of time together, we found we were unconsciously becoming connected.

There was excitement among us; the following day

we would be leaving Base Camp and heading down the mountain to recharge and replenish our tired bodies in the relatively oxygen-rich air of Dingboche village. We would stay there for three or four days to eat, hydrate, and sleep. I hoped to build back some fat reserves and recover from my now pronounced rib cage and shoulder bones. Before we set off, we each reviewed our condition and stats with the team at the Base Camp medical tent.

I felt weak from losing so much weight, and my cold had exploded my sinuses, which were completely blocked. I had lost all sense of taste and smell. My appetite had evaporated, and I had to consciously chew and swallow food. My throat throbbed; every swallow felt as if a razor blade was embedded in it. One of my fellow climbers was diagnosed with hemorrhoids, which was a serious issue. It was hard to manage pain, bleeding, and hygiene at altitude, and they were distraught at the diagnosis. Another had a cough that would not go away and which was draining a lot of their energy. Climbers have a name for this on Everest—the Khumbu cough, the cough that keeps on giving, and not in a good way. Having a cough above 7,000 meters (22,965 feet) is a concern because you can build intercostal muscle strain and single or multiple rib fractures can result, after which breathing can become an immensely painful experience. We would leave Base Camp a worn and bedraggled team.

The following morning we woke up at 7:30 a.m. to a clear blue sky and had a leisurely breakfast before organizing our sleeping bags and personal stuff to be carried down the mountain ahead of us by Sherpa porters. It felt like a true luxury to have only water and snacks in our backpacks—a featherweight compared to what we'd hauled up and down for the previous weeks. Considering how I felt, that suited me just fine.

After six hours of downhill trekking and almost 1,000 meters of descent, we arrived at Mingma's teahouse in Dingboche. She was waiting for us and gave each of us a motherly hug. She joked that we clearly didn't do well without her cooking. We needed fattening up, and she was the person to deliver. It was a surreal moment walking into this village again—not just recognizing how our physical and mental conditions had transformed us, but also when we compared what we knew now to the last time we'd been here almost a month before.

For our first meal, we were given menus beforehand and allowed our choice of food. A true novelty! We had all eaten the same food at Base Camp—no menu, just one dish for every meal. We laughed hysterically, and the jokes were flying. There we were, looking at a choice of sandwiches, salads, noodles, homemade French fries, and even home-made Nepalese-style pizza. Another luxury was taking a shower at Mingma's lodge— located in a drafty tin shed but with a bountiful supply of hot water. Being able to stand up fully, wash my body, and actually be clean—really clean—felt awesome. The greatest luxury, however, was not having to poop into a bag or squat between rocks on a glacier. The excitement and relief of sitting on a "throne" was precious—I'll never look at a toilet the same way again.

After dinner I lay in my sleeping bag on my plywood platform and slept solidly for almost eight hours. I woke up practically delirious from the unbroken sleep. It was as if my unconscious mind finally felt safe enough to allow me to sleep deeply and without any environmental awareness. I noticed the oxygen-rich air was also accelerating healing some cuts and blisters, which had been slow to recover at altitude. Science and the human body are infinitely wondrous and surprising.

Being at peace with yourself requires more than just the participation of the mind. The mind, the soul, and the body are all part of the same construct. Each needs the others, and each needs awareness and connection. All three are unique and need to be nurtured in their own ways.

This time in Dingboche was a chance to break free of the routine around which our days had been run so rigidly. There was no specific time for breakfast or lunch—only dinner, when we would eat together as a team. It was also an opportunity for me to recharge myself and clear my mind as well as my cold. It couldn't have come at a better time—colds are usually nothing more than an irritant at sea level, but on Everest they can mutate into a broader and more acute sickness. As my immune system was already compromised from exhaustion, weight loss, and the onset of the virus, I was worried it could deteriorate into a deeper sinus infection or pneumonia, so I needed that time to recuperate and, hopefully, turn the corner.

I did as little as possible for those few days in Dingboche—my most extravagant excursion was walking 300 meters to the internet café in the village, where I caught up on emails. My office manager back in New York City, Melissa, was holding the fort at the office, and my colleague Lillian was continuing my work with clients when they needed support. Most people knew I was away, so my inbox was light. It was more about responding to friends on Facebook and managing blog updates for Melissa to post. There were quite a few followers to what was my first blog ever, and it was inspirational to read some of the comments from friends, clients, and strangers alike. It felt unreal to think I was actually here.

The following day we had a visitor to the lodge. Dr. Peter Hackett was an accomplished physician famous for his research on the impact of altitude on the human body. He knew both Scott and Bill from their times in Alaska. He was also a respected mountaineer, having summited Everest in the early 1980s. He was heading the health clinic at Base Camp and was *the* go-to person for any question or topic about the human body on the highest mountain in the world. He joined us for lunch and spent a few hours in a relaxed and fascinating fireside-type chat. It was refreshing just to sit back and learn from someone new, and his style drew us in. He was a leader in his field who was humble yet open and assured in his delivery, and at the same time he asked about us. Openness to learning and growth is truly underrated.

The level of honesty and directness among the team members was pervasive now. Not to say that we had been purposefully holding back before, but people in general tend to put their best sides out as they get to know one another. Vulnerability is not shown until rapport and trust are established. We had gotten to know one another well in good times, and we'd also witnessed one another handle times of great fear, stress, and fatigue. During this, there was no place to hide. The openness led to humanity and a common language.

Scott was no longer playing the cheerleader, and we spoke openly about risk, the cost of mistakes, and how to think and work smarter. We discussed experiences and data points and had rational discussions around all scenarios for our upcoming summit rotation. It was immensely stimulating to know more about how the body works and reacts at exceptionally high altitudes.

One of the most interesting and entertaining discussions was about the various treatments for the symptoms of altitude sickness. Each of us had two drugs with us, that were recommended on Mountain Trip's gear list: Viagra and dexamethasone. Yes, that's right—Viagra on Everest. Not exactly a place known for romance. It's a highly effective vasodilator, meaning it increases the size of the arteries leading to the organs, those above the waist being its primary intention. Dexamethasone, on the other hand, is a strong steroid that also serves as treatment both for cerebral and pulmonary edemas—highly dangerous conditions that can cause rapid death at altitude. We chatted for hours until, having our fill of Q&A or perhaps Dr. Hackett more likely having his, we split up and went our separate ways until dinner. For a few hours we felt fully apprised of risk and the human condition.

On our last night in Dingboche, I entered the main room of the lodge and smelled burning yak dung coming from the stove—my cold was finally breaking and my sinuses were opening up. What a notable and memorable smell to proclaim my return to health.

To celebrate our recuperation in the green valley, Scott and Bill broke out a bottle of red wine, and we graciously accepted a glass of a beautiful Malbec to soothe our nerves ahead of our return to Base Camp the following day.

In the morning, after a hearty breakfast of pancakes, eggs, and toast, we packed up and said our final goodbyes to Mingma and her staff as she put blessed silk scarves around our necks. We would not be passing through Dingboche during our return to civilization. It was a strangely emotional moment—saying goodbye to someone who had been so good, so caring, and so generous to us, and someone we would likely never meet again in our lives. I left the village with a feeling of deep appreciation for the brave and warm people of these high mountain valleys. For a moment I heard the eloquent and poignant words of Anthony Bourdain recounting similar experiences meeting special people during his world travels.

The hike back to Base Camp was a notably quiet one; the familiar talk and chatter among the team was replaced by a visceral sense of excitement and anxiety. At a break in the trail, we heard through our radios about the first deaths on the mountain. Apparently, some teams were ascending the summit early, wanting to beat the crowds. With ropes not fully in place and the unstable weather, they succumbed on the upper slopes. It was a poignant reminder for us. All innocence had evaporated, and after two rotations we were now nakedly sober about what the climb involved and, more importantly, what would lie ahead.

CHAPTER 7

HURRY UP AND WAIT

AWAKING TO THE SUN'S DAWN rays warming my tent, I felt as though I had never left Base Camp. It was May 10 and Day 36 of our Everest expedition. With both excitement and trepidation, I walked over to the main tent. Inside it was akin to the Houston Space Center (at least our version of it), and it reminded me of a scene from *Apollo 13*. Scott and Bill had two laptops open, and there were pages of paper strewn in front of them with colorful weather charts, maps, and satellite images. Scott was on the radio communicating with some of our Sherpa team, who were higher up the mountain, carrying oxygen to the upper camps. His outward demeanor was calm as usual, but his brow was now furrowed and his concentration intense.

"Good morning, Scott here at Base Camp—how are you guys doing? Over."

The radio crackled. Everyone stared anxiously at the receiver.

Silence.

Scott tried again two more times.

After the third attempt, we heard a roaring wind over the radio, then a voice, heavily panting and out of breath.

"Good morning, we're okay . . . Over."

"Good to hear. Where are you guys now and what are the conditions? Over. How are the ropes and how far up have they been secured? Over."

"Weather not good. Very cold here. Making our way to Camp 4. Having tough time with ropes but hope to complete in next days. Over."

After lunch, Scott and Bill called a meeting and laid out the situation. They had been studying the different forecasts and assessing our options for our summit bid. The good news: a weather window was opening up on May 17, the first decent weather window for the season thus far. The concern, though, was that it was a narrow window with high winds of more than 130 kmh (80 mph), tapering only temporarily before regaining strength. Climbers ideally like to experience gusting winds of less than 50 kmh. Higher wind speeds—especially coming down, when the body would be at its weakest—meant an exponentially increased risk of hypothermia, frostbite, and, ultimately, death.

The next possible window was approximately five days later, although any weather window further out would obviously be less accurate and less reliable. This was further complicated by the different weather providers Scott was subscribing to, as each one had its own forecast about when the weather would change. Just like with hurricanes back home in the United States, we had to review a number of models to get a more complete picture of timing, opportunity, and risk. Three core weather elements were essential to the decision-making process and, indeed, our survival: wind, temperature, and precipitation.

Scott had pored over the data and was clearly tempted to go for the earlier window. Time was progressing, and the weather was changing with each day that passed, the air becoming more dense, humid, and unstable. The monsoon season was a massive seasonal occurrence for the whole Indian subcontinent, including the Himalayas, and we could feel it building around us in the increased intensity of the snowstorms at Base Camp. Another challenge was that we had no way of knowing if this would be the only weather window this season. With the change in climate over the previous four decades, nothing could be taken for granted.

Scott presented the options and trade-offs, then sat back and asked for questions, watching us carefully, clearly wanting to judge the mood of the group. Most of us were keen to go earlier and ideally maximize our chances, and the questions mostly reflected this. In typical Scott style, he was direct in his answers.

"Listen, I want to make sure we're on the same page here. Going early doesn't mean we have more options to summit. We have one shot at summiting, and there's no redo if we encounter difficulties or setbacks. If we commit to a date, that's our bid. If things don't work out, we will return down the mountain. I just want everyone to understand this." There it was, distilled into a crisp delivery—a wry slap back to reality for our ambitious and impatient minds.

After a few moments of silence, I asked, "What do *you* think we should do, Scott? What're your experience and intuition telling you?" He had been in this position multiple times before, and his experience mattered.

He stared back at me, taking a few seconds before responding, the emotion around making this tough call palpable. "I feel strongly that we should avoid this window and wait to see if another one opens up. There's just too much uncertainty, and the margins are too tight for my comfort level."

This was not a mountain in the Alps, where second attempts were commonly made. Climbing in the Death Zone was a game changer—everything was finite, including physical energy and oxygen supplies, and there would be no forgiveness for errors. On one level, the call was deflating and hard to swallow. Yet as a leader, Scott was delivering his tough message in a transparent, succinct, and assertive manner. And he showed his vulnerability through clearly feeling the stakes and impact of his opinion. It was not an ego decision of "I'm the leader so this is what I'm deciding." He was extremely smart putting out the facts and inviting our views and questions. It meant we had to consider the information before us and be brought into his world, where the data was inconclusive.

I could feel his comments drain the optimism that had been building since our recuperation at Dingboche. Outside in Base Camp, some other teams who had made the opposite decision were busy preparing to leave. We could hear and feel their intense excitement, and it only exaggerated our feeling of disappointment, their laughter punctuated by the call to action and in readying themselves for their departures up the mountain and into the weather.

Our dismay was undoubtedly also a result of our being there for so long already and our boredom, which was an ever-present threat to our mental and motivational health. It reminded me of war movies, where troops who had trained hard and prepared themselves felt that anyone leaving for danger before them was considered *lucky*. It's totally counterintuitive, but it's the way the human mind works, particularly under stress.

Emotion is the greatest seducer known to human-kind. Sometimes it's just really hard to separate the noise of momentum and excitement from reason. A crowd was moving up the mountain toward the glory of the summit, and it created a vortex of energy that was contagious and impossible to avoid. As is so often the case in life, it's the momentum of sentiment and emotion that moves stock markets, crowds, and hearts. Yet moving with the crowd here would have been a potential death wish for us. In truth, we would have been sheep, not heroes; all courage but no substance.

Analyze the data, focus on the purpose, and use the power of intuition. There are rarely perfect choices on mountains, just as there are rarely perfect paths in life. And to be clear, I'm not implying that our decision was better than any other team's decision to go up earlier than us. However, what was important was listening to *our* own judgment—judgment based on thoroughly gathering all the data possible so we could pore over it and understand what each piece and its implications meant. Then it was simply a matter of understanding what our whole purpose was. The emotion was saying to summit Everest, yet our overarching purpose was to return to our families—alive.

Intuition is perhaps our greatest superpower as humans. It's a gift we see in young children, where they can often be incredibly incisive and perceptive. Education, conditioning, and rational thinking can often teach us to second-guess such powers. Stranger still is that the power of emotion can often win the day. Faced with conflicting data, Scott's intuition—backed by his extensive experience and our trust in him—was crucial in making the call to wait. His main interest was for our safety, and whether we summited or not was less important than bringing us down the mountain in one piece. Decisions were being made not only around our goal but also around our survival. We didn't appreciate this fully at the time, but it grew in importance as the days progressed.

For the rest of the afternoon, we treated ourselves to two movies—*Ocean's 11* and *As Good as It Gets*. Clooney and Nicholson were the antidotes to disappointment, and we were soon laughing hard and unwinding through distraction. Humor is truly the oil that lubricates all wheels.

The following days moved painfully slowly, and it seemed the minutes and hours crawled by. We were conscious of not wasting energy on any more training, yet just being at Base Camp was detrimental to our health as we were back at altitude again. The recovery we made down in the valley was slowly ebbing away day by day.

After three days, we did a short three-hour hike to the nearby peak of Pumori, where we had a center-stage view of Everest's summit cone. It was the same spectacular sight we had seen on our hike in from Lukla, but this view was much closer. On the left side of the summit ridge, white ice plumes were blowing erratically off the glistening ice and rock. We knew this as a clear sign of strong winds and very cold and dangerous conditions. As we sat and ate our lunch on this peak, in our light jackets and without gloves, we realized that those who'd left a few days before would be walking into these conditions soon. It was a humbling moment, and one that tempered our impatience.

Just as we packed up our lunch, we bumped into the climbing team including Russell Brice from Discovery Channel's *Everest: Beyond the Limit*. We hadn't seen them at all before now, even though they were a large group. Their camp had been a self-imposed quarantine zone, and it literally had skull and crossbones signs forbidding entry for all but their team members. This was their way to control their health by limiting any imported virus or bug risk. I was surprised and extremely happy to meet two Danes with whom I had climbed in Antarctica: Jens, a solid climber and a man of few words, and Stina, a tall Viking-blonde woman who was usually the life of the expedition but who was uncharacteristically subdued and measured now. We chatted for a while and she shared how life in her team quarantine was tough; it was a competitive group with very strong climbers. It felt like they weren't having the same bonding experience we were having within our team. Perhaps it was because the group was large, or maybe they were just a collection of people and personalities who did not jive well.

The guides chatted about their similar decision to wait it out for now. As they scanned the summit ridge and the weather conditions, I could feel their collective sense of relief but also an anxiousness about how many people would end up making the later summit bid, and how this would impact our safety. With the unstable weather situation, it was looking likely that a decent number of the twenty-one climbing teams on the mountain would be leaving for the summit at approximately the same time—chasing the same weather window. There is no central coordination of climbing on Everest; each team makes its own decisions and schedule. So there would likely be a crowding problem.

The following days passed slowly. Some other teams were packing up and leaving Base Camp for the valley below, their expeditions coming to an end as they viewed the weather window as being too tight. Most upsetting was the stark reminder of the perils that lay ahead for each of us as the glacier released more bodies below the Icefall. The body of a Sherpa called Phinjo was recovered in the lower

Icefall, near the first ladders. A highly experienced climber, Phinjo had been on his ninth expedition climbing a mountain over 8,000 meters with two other Sherpa in April 2006 when they were killed in an ice collapse, and the glacier subsumed their bodies. Apparently, the remains would be carried back to Phortse, where they would be received by the family and then cremated.

Scott and Bill continued to watch the weather in obsessive detail multiple times a day. We heard reports that some of the earlier-departed teams had pushed up toward the summit, while others were now retreating down the mountain due to the weather. Multiple incidences of frostbite injuries, which are particularly associated with summit attempts, accompanied these reports. Problems with hydration, fatigue, delays, and hypothermia all contribute to a breakdown in circulation that normally flushes the fingers, toes, and extremities with warm blood in response to getting cold.

One of the worst cases was a climber who made a critical decision to bivouac (sleep outside) just below the South Col because he felt too exhausted to walk the last 100 meters to camp. According to a report from Dr. Hackett posted on May 20, 2010, on the blog at alanarnette.com,

> He slept on a rock, apparently attached to the fixed line, and somehow lost the mitten glove on his right hand during the night. He was climbing alone, his "teammates" apparently unaware of his location and he had no Sherpa support. Amazingly, he survived the night out without a tent, sleeping bag, stove to make water, or any help. In the morning, he ascended to Camp 4 on the South Col and there

A storm brewing on the Lhotse Face.
Courtesy of Scott Woolums.

Camp 3: our perch halfway up the Lhotse Face.

Sherpa helping change out my oxygen tank
on the Lhotse Face.

Cindy and I rising above all surrounding peaks into the
upper atmosphere. Courtesy of Bill Allen.

The spectacularly barren and wild South Col.
Courtesy of Bill Allen.

Me topping out of the Geneva Spur. Courtesy of Bill Allen.

Oxygen bottles stacked at the South Col.
Courtesy of Cindy Abbott.

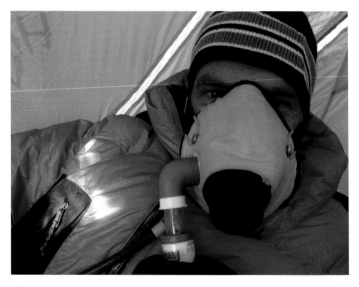

Final hours before our summit bid marathon.
Courtesy of Ania Lichota.

Pensive moments at the South Col while watching the weather below us. Courtesy of Ania Lichota.

Cold feet and frostbite fears as dawn breaks.
Courtesy of Paul Fejtek.

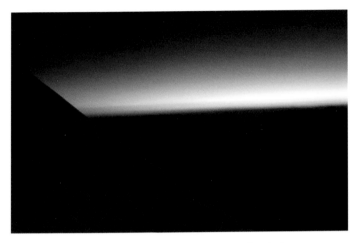

From the summit cone of Everest, a new day is born, while we witness the curvature of the earth. Inspiration and humility.

The cone gets dramatically steeper as we push toward the summit ridge. Courtesy of Scott Woolums.

Looking across the cornice/knife-edge at the infamous Hillary Step, my emotions breaking. Courtesy of Bill Allen.

Final meters to the summit. Courtesy of Scott Woolums.

Reaching the top of the world on Day 47: May 23, 9:23 a.m. Courtesy of Scott Woolums.

Exhausted—physically and emotionally—at the summit.

Below us, the entire planet. Above us, space.

My broken and empty gaze at the South Col.
Courtesy of Ania Lichota.

Our guardians: a Sherpa lookout on the Lhotse Face.
Courtesy of Bill Allen.

Snow angel time—childhood returns.

Smile and party like a Sherpa.

The body of a climber who died the previous season is recovered. Courtesy of Ania Lichota.

Flight to freedom and warm showers.
Courtesy of Ania Lichota.

received help in starting back down. A physical exam showed severe frostbite to his hands and to his ears, but no frostbite of the toes, a testimonial to the quality of his boots. The next morning a helicopter took him to Kathmandu. The next day there were three more cases of severe frostbite, relating to questionable decision-making, hypoxia, and dehydration. One climber decided to stop at the Balcony on the way up, at about 8,400 meters. He was moving too slowly and was very fatigued. He decided to wait for his teammates, while they continued on to the summit. They returned five to six hours later. His immobilization at such altitude cost him most of his toes and one finger.

Finally, just after lunch on May 17, we got sudden word that the weather window was happening. Scott and Bill entered the main tent, and the decision was made to move up later that evening—for a summit bid on May 23 and 24. In Scott's view, it would take us five days to get up and two days to get down. There was immediate excitement and relief—we would have our chance to launch our final rotation.

We'd been in standby mode for days, so we had little packing to do, but Scott still took the time to review what each of us was planning to take up. There was no plan B for equipment. Any clothing or supplies missing from here on could have a huge impact, so we had to get it right. To our surprise, Scott handed out strips of yellow plastic reflector tape—it was his MacGyver solution to us being able to recognize one another uniquely as a team in the darkness or in a storm. He gave specific direction as to where he wanted us to affix them to our gear and backpacks.

I went to bed excited but also feeling a clear undercurrent of anxiety. I would be entering a physical and mental environment I had never experienced before, and though we planned as much as we could, many aspects would be out of our control. Although I had strong confidence in my determination and drive, this was a lonely, scarier feeling—as if drive alone wouldn't be enough.

PART 3

THE SUMMIT
RECKONING

CHAPTER 8

BREAKING FOR THE SOUTH COL

At 1:15 A.M., my alarm went off and I bolted upright in the tent. Despite having slept restlessly for just three or four hours, the adrenaline quickly kicked in. I finished packing and zipping while listening to the Sherpa gathering outside. My hands shook as I tied my backpack strings tight, even though I didn't have any particular thoughts in my mind beyond closing up my pack.

At 3:00 a.m., we assembled quietly. There was a tempered enthusiasm as we circled the puja chorten (altar) three times, while our head Sherpa, Dawa, burned juniper twigs and recited Buddhist prayers. There was an intensity around him as he blessed each of us by wafting the juniper around our heads and shoulders, as if he were directing the blessings of the gods for the dangers ahead. In the flickering light of my headlamp, the faces of my fellow climbers and Sherpa looked pale, yet the focus in their eyes was clear and steely. The entire Base Camp Sherpa support team appeared out of the darkness, in their sweatpants and thick down jackets, to quietly witness our departure and wish us well. They had been there for us every day the past five weeks, and now they had gotten up just to see us off. I was immediately moved by the sight.

This display of Sherpa solidarity was so unexpected and unannounced. They were celebrating our takeoff for the summit and understood very clearly our purpose and their contributions. I hadn't even thought of it beforehand. But ever since, I have reflected on the profound significance our impact has on others, both conscious and unconscious. This wasn't just about shared purpose, although that is important and invaluable. It's human nature to be part of a tribe and to feel connected. People have a deep preference to build rapport with one another, including during times when we may have different views and opinions. There's a sense of humanity, which most of us share and seek. These are both the building blocks and the glue to any relationship.

True rapport is not created by crowing about what I stand for or what I believe in or what I want. It's much smarter than that, but it's also simpler. It's about creating followership, which is pulled by people, not pushed into them. Whether we set ourselves as an example for what we espouse, speak with passion and conviction rather than with ultimatums, or engage with people to make them feel heard and valued, the formula is clear. We impact people with what we say and do, whether we mean to or not, so it's easier to take ownership of this and be aware of it by being aware of ourselves first. It's an arc with assertive accountability on one end of the spectrum and humble acceptance on the other.

We left our quiet supporters at Base Camp and like a Navy SEAL team, we moved into the darkness in unison for our third and final ascent through the Icefall. The air was still, the night bitterly cold. However, we soon warmed up as we found our steady rhythm. Entering the Icefall's popcorn of ice boulders, I looked ahead and saw a line of headlamps snaking its way upward. A number of other teams had left Base Camp just before us, and we were all progressing steadily through the dark maze. The moon was bright and its reflective light off the ice created a surreal monochrome scene of twilight and shadows.

Just after 4:00 a.m., light from the horizon slowly illuminated the peaks around us, and we turned off our headlamps. The Icefall had changed, and the route was markedly different from our second rotation almost two weeks ago. As we approached the upper fall, we heard rumblings of ice breaking free. A mini avalanche tumbled to our left. We continued forward without stopping—smoothly, assertively, and with few words between us.

As we rose over the last ice block, having made it through in about four hours, we saw the red livery of a Nepalese air force helicopter passing over us. This pilot would be back in Kathmandu within an hour, I thought, and that night would sleep deeply in his or her own warm bed. I imagined what that felt like. My drifting thoughts were broken when I realized it was flying unusually slowly. The roar of the engine said it was close to its maximum thrust, laboring at this altitude to gain height. Helicopters use their rotating blades to push air downward against the force of gravity to stay airborne. One thing that allows this to happen is the density of air. Base Camp has half the oxygen as the amount at sea level, and at the summit this was reduced to 33 percent. So in a weird sense, a machine such as a helicopter suffers similarly to humans—with a limit of its performance and an exponentially increased chance of catastrophe.

After a snack break at Camp 1, we left for the Western Cwm, which became a furnace when the sun hit the floor of the valley. I had to strip down to a thin-layer top and roll my sleeves up. It felt like *Groundhog Day*, although I was more concerned about managing my hydration this time because any weakness would impact my energy for the tough days to follow. About forty minutes into the hike, there was a huge crevasse to cross—so big, in fact, that we nicknamed it the "Grand Canyon." We each had to step down a ladder and into a ravine to be able even to access it. As I reached it, clouds passed over the sun and it became extremely cold. I quickly put on my down jacket and thick gloves. There was a line of climbers and Sherpa waiting to cross, and for good reason. The movement of the glacier had pulled away the left-side rope overnight, and it was now almost impossible to reach. It was a real-time dilemma on how to cross safely.

After a wait, I finally reached the front of the line. Normally, each person crossing the ladder waits to lift the slack ropes off the snow that act as handrails and hold them taut for the person following. We had perfected this as a team in previous rotations. However, I was the first member of my team to cross this time. As I looked across, the person before me was gone. The thin ropes lay bare. I tried to grab the left rope with my trekking pole, stretching past my comfort zone. After missing it a couple of times, I finally hooked the rope and pulled it back to grab with my hand, which stretched it extremely taut. As I grabbed the right-side rope, I noticed that I was lopsided on the ladder. I felt anger building in my head about the other person not waiting and leaving me in this position.

The ladder itself was not one but three ladders strapped together with flimsy string to make it reach across the 6-meter-wide crevasse perhaps 40 to 50 meters deep. It creaked and bounced like a rubber band with every movement of my body. I wobbled as I tried to stay balanced, my core being stretched. About two-thirds of the way across, I could no longer keep it together. I lost my balance. Turning my body like a pretzel, I crashed down on the ladder in kneeling position. My heart leapt and I immediately felt a shot of adrenaline explode through my entire body. The pain of landing on my knee-caps forced out an expletive. The sudden jerk released my water bottle from the side of my backpack. It bounced off the jagged glasslike sides of the crevasse, emitting a *ping, ping, ping* for what sounded like a mini eternity before going quiet.

I gripped the ladder tightly in the downward dog position, bracing for the collapse of the shaking ladder or my loss of balance that would tip me over into the dark crevasse. I couldn't avoid looking down into the black hole below me. My lungs were hyperventilated, my body in full shock mode.

Slowly, the ladder steadied, then stopped moving. At that moment, the clouds cleared and the sun and its heat blasted the gully. In my down jacket and thick hat, with my heart racing, I started sweating profusely. Memories of the earlier ladder crossings raced through my mind. I couldn't stay here.

I heard the voices of my colleagues behind me: "Vivian, don't stop—keep moving, you're almost there!"

I stretched out with my arms and pulled myself forward, moving one knee at a time, one stretch at a time, and finally reached the end of the ladder. I heard claps from people around me and felt a collective sense of relief, none greater than my own.

Reaching the other side of the gully, I found a place to sit and put my head in my hands. My heart was thumping, and I felt every muscle in my body shaking. It felt like post-traumatic shock, but there was no time to process. We needed to keep moving. Within a minute, I was climbing the vertical ladder out of the gully to get back onto the Cwm for the long walk to Camp 2.

The shock of the near accident had drained me physically and mentally, and I labored for a while, trying to shake off the experience so vivid in my mind. At a break, I sat down, sipped water from another flask, and closed my eyes to clear my head. When I opened them, a butterfly was looking at me. I had to do a double take. Its wings were a kaleidoscope of red, orange, black, and blue colors, and it had landed on my red backpack. It seemed bizarre for something so delicate to be present at this height, in a desert of snow, ice, and rock, but it brought me peace and cleared my mind. If a butterfly could be here, perhaps I could too. Later I learned that butterflies migrate over the Himalayas, which made me wonder whether we were both being challenged and tested.

As we got within sight of the camp, Cindy was doing poorly. She was feeling weak and having to rest every few hundred meters. We chatted about counting steps to one hundred, to distract her mind and keep her body moving. Later she felt worse, and it became clear she was suffering from heat exhaustion. Ania called Scott on the radio and a Sherpa was dispatched from Camp 2 to bring liquids and help carry her backpack to camp. The lighter load and refreshments helped, and not long after, she made it to camp and we closed out our first summit rotation day. It had been a day of drama, and I eagerly crawled into my sleeping bag after dinner and fell asleep within seconds.

The following day was one of temporary rest and recuperation. The plan was to leave very early the following morning for Camp 3, so I spent the afternoon organizing my pack. Camp 2 had become our "advanced base camp," and it was a staging post for the summit attempt, so any equipment fine-tuning and weight distribution of the pack would be done here. I also used that day to update my blog and inform those back home that we were on our way up. With the sudden departure from Base Camp, I didn't have time to get that done before, so I felt relieved. From there on, there would be no laptops, only radios and Scott's satellite phone, which would have limited availability. In a sense, we were leaving the very few creature comforts we'd gotten used to behind. We would be less connected and more exposed than we had ever been before.

We left camp at 5:00 a.m., fully packed and ready for the ascent halfway up the Lhotse Face to Camp 3. The weather was cold and breezy, and we were wearing our full-body-length suits now. Akin to an astronaut suit, its sole purpose was to keep us warm with thick goose down filling and insulation throughout. The downside was that it was bulky, hard to maneuver in, and awkward to pee from—and this is me talking as a guy.

As dawn arrived and we got close to the base of the ice face, we noticed a long line of antlike dots on the face itself. That was the group we could be summiting with— those who, similar to us, had judged the initial window to be too small and unreliable. It was disconcerting to see the number of people; that meant delays and a slower ascent ahead. At the foot of the ice face, Scott told us to take a break and have a snack. He and Bill walked away a few meters, surveyed upward, and got on the radio. Looking up, we could see clearly only for a few hundred meters. Beyond that were clouds, plumes of ice crystals, and snow blowing off the glistening slopes. Clearly, it was more than breezy up there, and the sun was completely hidden. We were already feeling the cold in our sheltered position at the base and wanted to get moving.

After twenty minutes, Scott came over and we had a team huddle.

"I've never seen this wind on the ice face, and I'm not a fan of getting frozen in a slow line up to Camp 3 and then enduring a stormy night on a narrow snow ledge. I think we should wait another day at Camp 2 and see if things are calmer tomorrow." His words made sense—the conditions were clearly far from ideal, but the setback still deflated me immensely. My body had been on this mountain for almost six weeks, and the idea of extending it by even one more day was an exhausting thought. That was compounded by the fact that the first cyclone of the season was moving in from the Bay of Bengal. Named Cyclone Laila, the storm had formed on May 17 and was reported to be rapidly intensifying—a term referring to a rapid drop in barometric pressure, which usually coincides with a sharp increase in winds and precipitation. Both weather elements were bad news for Everest, and my mind swirled. What would happen if this loss of a day meant we missed our window and the cyclone shut down the mountain? To have come so far, to be so close, and to have put all our effort on the line took me back to missing the first weather window a week ago and my deep sense of disappointment.

Upon hearing Scott's news, Ania shouted with joy—she had been recovering from a stomach virus for a few days and had labored all morning to get this far. She told me later that she had been seriously thinking today could have been her turn back day, so a disappointment for me was a reprieve for her, and that felt more than okay.

As we reached camp, I looked back and saw the entire ice face enveloped in clouds—perhaps we were safer staying there after all. After dropping our packs, we decided to get lost in a long card game, and before long the laughs and smiles returned. It's interesting how distraction and humor are effective anesthetics to changing negative states that would otherwise multiply and deepen.

The following morning was the perfect weather day—a cloudless sky without even a trace of wind. As we surveyed the ice face, we saw plenty of empty space and only a handful of climbers. We left camp with renewed but tender optimism.

This time we stopped at the base for just ten minutes before clambering up the steep chimneys and launching ourselves onto the ice. Ania had recovered, and we made good progress together as a team. The reflective sunlight off the ice made it dangerously bright. This, combined with the altitude and the thin atmosphere, meant the UV level was incredibly powerful. Any exposed skin unprotected by sunscreen would be quickly burned and severely damaged, even more so with my pale Celtic skin. An even bigger danger was snow blindness, which is an excruciatingly painful condition when the sun burns through your cornea. It happens when you take off your sunglasses, usually due to them fogging up, and carelessly leave them off. Brightness at this altitude is ten to fifteen times over the safe limit for the human eye. I kept my glasses firmly on and tried to reapply my sunscreen every two hours—an awkward task on a steep, glasslike slope.

After some grueling hours, I finally saw some color just above us that I soon recognized as the first tents of Camp 3. My excitement was tempered when Scott passed word down the line that our tents were at the upper end of camp, meaning another thirty minutes of climbing. The extra effort allowed a higher-level start the following morning and, hopefully, a chance to get ahead of the other teams camping just below us. However, the extra climb felt like an eternity as it got steeper and steeper, finally ending up on a 60- to 70-degree pitch. I could no longer see tents and wondered if Scott had been underselling the effort. Finally, off to my right, I saw a large serac of snow and ice and, just behind, a tiny ledge where our distinctive orange tents seemed to cling for dear life. Our Sherpa team had brought up the tents the day before to establish our temporary encampment. I seriously wondered how wise it was to stay there. There was literally not 1 centimeter of space between the edge of the tent and the side of the ice face—a steep drop and a slide of almost 1,000 meters!

The camp was so dangerous it had its own rules for us:

1. If we left our tent, we must be clipped into the safety rope at all times. The safety rope was secured with screws driven into the ice.
2. During the night, we were not allowed to leave the tent. All toilet needs were to be managed inside the tent and waste stored until morning.

Over the years, a number of climbers have slipped to their deaths while taking a toilet break, many disappearing into the crevasses far below, never to be seen again. Not exactly a glamorous way to go.

I was sharing a tent with Ania again, so we had the "chat." It was agreed that we would use our pee bags in the tent itself, as we had done before during the nights. However, if we needed to go for a number 2, we would use the small vestibule of the tent (the narrow space between the outer shell and the inner shell). Obviously, this option at night amid the freezing temps was a miserable and unpleasant thought for both parties, but we had to be clear about how we'd work it.

After clipping ourselves onto the rope and holding a bowl of ramen in our hands, we sat back against the ice wall and savored the view before us. The sky was clear, the air was still, and the entire vista was mesmerizing as the sun set in slow motion in front of us. At that altitude of 7,400 meters, the view seemed limitless, and with so little atmosphere, the orange horizon was perfectly clear. For a few lazy seconds, my brain associated this view with a mountain village in the Alps as I was surveying the scenery after a day on the ski slopes. After a few minutes, we were throwing around metaphors; the best suited came with "the calm conditions matched the *Titanic* enjoying its pondlike Atlantic Ocean on the night of April 15, 1912— before it met its iceberg and rapid demise." We soaked up the atmosphere and ate our tasteless food. It would be all dried foods and heat-ups from this point on.

After dinner we received our oxygen masks and tanks for the very first time. At that altitude, we were on the cusp of the Death Zone. It was a significant change to have something constantly stuck to my face for the days and nights ahead, though a lifesaving inconvenience. In the months before my departure for Everest, people asked me whether I'd be climbing with or without oxygen. The answer was obvious. The body desperately needs it in this extreme environment, primarily to maintain cognitive function but also for circulation—to reduce the threat of frostbite.

That meant trying to sleep with a bulky and awkward oxygen mask on and a large oxygen tank nearby. I dozed for about thirty minutes before waking up with my heart pounding. I was exhausted but couldn't sleep. I could hear the constant hissing of the oxygen from the valve on the mask. My heart was racing even with the supplemental oxygen, and I couldn't seem to relax with this thing on my face. Whenever I did doze off for even a few minutes, my unconscious mind played games associated with the precariousness of our tents. I imagined myself slipping off our perch and free-falling down the ice. It was a ridiculous thought, but altitude does that to you—rational thoughts are no longer in command and irrational ones invade at will and hemorrhage energy. Ania seemed to be in the same position: restless, waking repeatedly, napping rather than sleeping. It was a long night.

Eventually my watch reached 3:00 a.m. and we slowly pulled ourselves up and out of our sleeping bags. Bill came around with boiling water and we hydrated our dry oatmeal. I tried my best to swallow despite my lack of appetite. Adrenaline surged through my body, compensating for the sleep deprivation. At just after 4:00 a.m., I tightened my harness and lifted up my backpack. I looked like a hybrid between an astronaut and a fighter pilot; my big down suit had increased my body contour size by 50 percent and the oxygen mask had taken over a large part of my face and jaw. The mask was connected to a hose, which led to an aluminum cylinder of air that was stuffed into my backpack.

It was getting bright as we walked across our tiny ledge to the 70-degree ice wall. The angle of ascent looked ridiculous—the nearest thing to climbing onto a sheer rock face made of ice. Unfortunately, we were not alone—there was a long line of perhaps eighty climbers already on the fixed lines, and we waited as if on the ramp feeding into a freeway. The morning air was extremely cold, and we were in our full down suits.

It was a very steep climb for about forty-five minutes before we turned left to cross the "gun barrel"—a chute between two ridges, which looked to be about 70 meters wide. The downward side was a long, smooth, and very steep ice slide for hundreds of meters to Camp 3. A climber ahead of us who was crossing it shuffled their backpack; their water bottle came loose and it took off down the slide, picking up phenomenal velocity. The sight transfixed everyone standing in line. A human body would be no slower in its tumble down the mountain. That was not a place to make a mistake. When it was my turn, I stepped across and onto the thin path worn into the ice. I angled my boots in an awkward sideways position on the slope while trying to balance and negotiate the anchor reclipping transition. It was nerve-wracking, and even though I tried to avoid looking down to my left, I intuitively felt the sudden vacuum of space as I inched my way across the gap.

On the other side, we climbed upward again and were soon greeted by the growing flickers of sunshine as the rays came over the ridge far above us. I felt a surge of energy as I recognized the sun like an old friend, replacing darkness with light as the nascent warmth touched the skin on my face. I basked in this positive feeling for a good twenty minutes before the warmth slowly turned to sweat, and that led to a growing fear. My full-length down suit needed to stay on at all times to protect against the weather changes that can happen within seconds. To triage the temperature fluctuations, I had to be conscious about zipping and unzipping my suit and the all-important side vents, which allowed cooler air to circulate. My level of sweat and dehydration had a direct correlation to how much I needed to drink. Water is heavy to carry, and I had only a finite amount. One aims to carry the right amount with a slight margin—that's it. Running out would mean dehydration and the cascading effects that would have on my health.

Above us now was the Yellow Band—a famous bank of rock about 100 meters in length with a yellow hue. It looks like a minor obstacle, but in reality it's an energy-sapping challenge. This was basically the first time we were climbing on rock since leaving Base Camp, and herein lay the problem. We were wearing crampons, and once a crampon touches a rock, it slides. It was totally impractical to try to remove our crampons on such a steep section, so we had to pull ourselves up with the rope while trying to find every nook and crack in the rock for our crampons to maintain some grip and move up. It was a huge effort since arms were involved now. I tried to haul my body up and felt the throbbing as my wasted arm muscles strained to support my body weight. It felt like my best effort resulted in three steps up and two steps sliding back down.

Our progress was painfully slow and hugely draining. The noise of multiple sets of crampons scraping and sliding on the rocks amplified our frustration and sheer effort. After thirty minutes, I finally climbed over the last section and my boots landed reassuringly on the ice. Exhausted, I panted incessantly for air, despite being on oxygen. At the next anchor point, I unhitched my backpack and increased the flow rate from the cylinder valve. As I looked upward, the line and the obstacles looked endless. I started to fret about how much longer I could maintain this pace with this level of fatigue.

After another hour, I was laboring and began worrying why I was so tired. One of our Sherpa came and helped me change the oxygen tank on the trail. It was a tricky exercise—I had to lean over to allow him access to swap out the cylinders from my backpack. However, the new tank didn't seem to help. I continued to feel drained for the rest of the day.

The Geneva Spur was the last obstacle of the day, a long trail of rock and ice leading up to a very steep and exposed ridge. On the other side lay Camp 4—Everest's infamous South Col. The ascent was slow and steady to the base of the Spur, where we had to wait for our turn to ascend. I craned my neck upward, staring in awe at the fierce beauty in front of us—300 meters of sheer incline. The steepness and rapid ascent to almost 8,000 meters was our separation into the upper atmosphere, like when a space rocket jettisons its heavy fuel tankers as it approaches the Earth's atmosphere. The Spur represented a transition, and it seemed like we were suddenly above almost everything around us. The sky was eliciting a different shade of blue, the atmosphere glowed against the horizon, and the light was sharper and brighter than I had ever seen. Each step was a massive effort, and my calves and thighs burned in unison. As we approached the top, it got so steep we were crawling on hands and knees. With Cindy close behind me and an empty space around us, it felt for a while like we were the only two people on the mountain.

Finally, we reached the lip of the ridge where Bill was waiting with encouraging words and his video camera. The dark pyramid of Everest's summit cone soared into the heavens before us. Its scale and might were palpable. The dark rock and plumes of ice crystals blowing off its upper reaches, combined with the howling of the jet stream, added to the brooding atmosphere above.

After almost eight hours of toil, we arrived at Camp 4 at 12:30 p.m. Having read stories about Everest since childhood, I was moved by the experience. The South Col seemed to be the place of ultimate drama—the final staging post for a summit ascent as well as the first point of relative safety after descending the treacherous slopes or through abominable weather. In my wildest dreams, I had never imagined I'd actually be there.

The only plateau or place of relative flatness on the upper slopes of the mountain, the South Col was about the size of two soccer pitches, and the camp was a desolate, raw, and windswept place. Our small group of orange tents sat buffeted by the blustery wind, stashes of oxygen cylinders stacked neatly into a pyramid beside them. Our amazing Sherpa team had carried up all this equipment and all these supplies in the days and weeks before we arrived to be ready for this moment. It was a humbling realization.

The aluminum poles of a tent left from a previous season stood like a naked ribcage, its tent material bleached by the powerful UV rays and shredded by the hurricane winds that typically inhabited this altitude. I mused about what could have happened and the crisis that must have ensued for this lifesaving equipment to have been abandoned here, of all places.

I crawled into my own tent and sat with Ania, who had

arrived more than an hour ahead of me. For the most part we were speechless, our eyes reflecting the truth about what it had taken to get here and what still lay ahead. I ached all over, and the exhaustion was almost overwhelming. Too tired to sleep, I lay back and looked up at the flapping ceiling of the tent, appreciating that I didn't have to move any part of my body.

I felt terrible. What had been a slight headache earlier now throbbed with increasing intensity, and I felt nauseous. Summoning the energy to go to Scott's tent, I returned with the satellite phone and took some minutes to compose myself before calling my office phone to leave a voicemail. I had agreed with my assistant that she would post voice-mails on the blog to inform the many people following me. I didn't have the energy to call my family and worried that if I did, they would ask questions about my condition, and I would have to answer them. The voicemail, where I could control the message, was a better alternative. I dialed the number, took deep breaths of oxygen, and steeled myself before recording the following:

> Greetings from Camp 4, South Sol, Mount Everest. We made it here after seven and a half hours. We got up at 3:00 a.m. this morning and had a few tricky pieces on the way. We were on oxygen the whole way. Had a beautiful day. It started off really cold and then got very warm in our down suits. It's now just after 1:00 in the afternoon and we're going to try and get some sleep for five or six hours and get up at 7:00, then get ready and probably leave at 9:00 p.m. for the summit. So, it's going to be a big day. We're pretty tired but we'll

recharge and we're in good shape. We seem to have a weather window so we're hoping the gods will be with us for tonight and tomorrow, and we'll crack the summit! Thanks for all good wishes and hope to have some good news tomorrow! Vivian, signing out from the South Col of Mount Everest. Take care.

The message was a sham. I was not physically in good shape, my spirits were low, and the weather was far from optimal. Plus, I wasn't going to get much or any sleep ahead of our departure.

The one thing I had a lot of time to think about since my legacy epiphany at Base Camp was how every word from me mattered to others. My family and friends were equally anxious for me, and if anything were to happen to me that night, that voicemail would be my last, one they would pore over for eternity. It's OK to be both strong and vulnerable at the same time. In fact, when you peel back the layers, they are one and the same. The only choice is who you want to be. I wanted my voice and tone to be positive and upbeat. This was the conundrum. The expedition had opened me up like a can, and I was feeling more open and real, but this openness could impact and unduly upset others. I had to dig deep for the one minute it took to record that voicemail.

As I ended the call, tears welled up in my eyes. Truth was, for the first time on the mountain, I was scared for my life.

CHAPTER 9
THE SUMMIT MIRROR

NOT LONG AFTER I recorded my last blog voicemail before the summit attempt, Scott and Bill came to our tent. Scott had a sullen look on his face.

"We've been studying the weather, and it's complicated. We could try and go for the summit tonight, as was our plan, but it's too windy and dangerously cold. Or we could wait until tomorrow and see if the weather improves. The latest reports on the cyclone say it's getting closer to us, and we could start feeling the effects anytime in the next twenty-four hours. So there are no good choices right now. As we've discussed, our single most important goal is to get down this mountain safely. In this weather, we cannot move, and I've made the decision for us to stay here tonight. We will reassess tomorrow. Any questions?"

For the first time, there were no questions for Scott. It was clear there was only one choice. I was relieved by not having to move. I spent the rest of the afternoon trying to hydrate and doing my best to get any amount of sleep.

A couple of hours later, at 5:00 p.m., there was a commotion outside, and I heard a bunch of voices. Suddenly Bill peered into the tent.

"How are you guys doing?" he asked. "You may have noticed that the wind has reduced here in the last two hours, so we've decided that tonight is likely our only summit opportunity. We're going to go for it, so you need to get yourselves ready. We will leave in two hours."

I looked at Ania and we both exhaled and exclaimed the same expletive. This was Mountaineering 101, and I had experienced it multiple times before—having to react to the conditions in real time, constantly evolving and adapting. I'd slept maybe thirty minutes the whole afternoon. In hindsight, I was running a massive sleep deficit— sleeping only five hours in three days—and it was taking a toll on my body.

As the light faded into twilight, I went outside to take a toilet break. At the South Col, there were no defined toilet areas, so I walked over to some rocks and squatted. During my cleanup phase, I noticed a female climber, about 20 meters away, in the same phase. Our glances met and, as if in a Monty Python skit, we acknowledged each other with a nod and continued on with *our business*. In a matter of months, Everest had been able to break down the internal social barriers that we had built up over our conditioned lives to reduce us to this level of openness and vulnerability. Just two people trying to survive in the Death Zone.

As I walked back to the tent, I looked down the hill and saw a thick layer of cloud. I realized that, at almost 8,000 meters (5 miles above sea level), we were in the upper atmosphere. Below this cloud, the daily snowstorms we had gotten used to at Base Camp were happening live. We were truly above the weather.

Ania and I prepared some ramen (yet again), and I had to force myself to eat and swallow. My body was not happy, signaling its difficulty accepting food and an inability to digest at this altitude. There was just not enough oxygen in my body to support normal digestion. I tried a chocolate bar and the taste was the same—nothing. My taste buds had lost all sensitivity.

Getting ready was an exercise in slow motion. I had decided to have my toilet break without oxygen, and it took ten minutes for my breathing to recover back in the tent. Slowly preparing our gear, we went into autopilot mode, running through our pre-climb checklist, which had been prepared so many times before. This time, though, we needed each other. I looked over at Ania; she was having trouble doing the all-important double-back strap pull on her waist harness—a fatal error if she lost her footing and the harness came undone in a fall. I helped her secure it. A few minutes later, I was wrestling to put on my boots and was über-focused on keeping the stiff plastic tongue of the boot open before trying to fit my right foot inside.

"Vivian, wrong boot," she called out. "Right boot for your right foot!"

Despite experience and muscle memory, mistakes were starting to happen as our cognitive functions faltered. We needed one another now more than ever.

At 8:15 p.m., our team gathered together outside in complete darkness. I looked up and could see a long line of headlamps heading up the steep pyramid—a foreboding sight. We would have one Sherpa climbing with each of us for the summit bid as support, should any incidents happen. Scott pulled us together in a circle with our Sherpa and spoke.

"This will be our last climb upward and what we have been working toward for the last two months. Above all, we honor safety and communication. As we have done on

155

every climb up to now, we make decisions as a team. Stay close and look out for the unique reflective markers we put on your packs and suits. Next stop is the Balcony."

We left the camp in absolute silence, full of uncertainty and anxiety, our absolute focus on placing one boot in front of the next. The air was clear, and the sky was lit with a kaleidoscope of stars. It looked like the whole sky was in 3D, perhaps because we were closer to it now. The climbing from the get-go was steep. Initially, the trail took us through chimneylike gullies of packed snow and ice, where we needed to pull ourselves up on the fixed line with the help of our ascender devices. I could feel the limited remains of my energy as I pulled the rope to lift myself upward; my arms received little reprieve as the ascender locked in place. As we progressed, various additional obstacles came before us—rock formations that had to be climbed and navigated, and smaller loose rocks and ice debris, some of which came loose and caused havoc down the line.

After an hour, we found ourselves moving at a snail's pace with long stops as the line of people ground to a halt before starting again. One such stop lasted more than thirty minutes. With no coordinated communication down the line whatsoever, it was unclear what was happening, and frustration began to build. I was standing in a fixed position on a steep incline, so in addition to getting cold, my feet and leg muscles were starting to strain and tire. Some climbers couldn't handle it and unclipped themselves from the safety of the line and snaked upward past us, to our left side—effectively free climbing with certain death if they fell.

With as many climbers below us as above us, we were firmly in the middle of the jam. As time went by, two individuals came down our fixed line. The first was delirious and wobbling, while the other, his Sherpa, looked exhausted trying to manage him as they unclipped and reclipped painfully slowly at each anchor point. The climber was likely suffering from pulmonary edema—his eyes were glazed over, and he was mumbling incoherently to himself as he slowly passed me. Within the next thirty minutes, two more sick climbers followed, their expedition over. Their only goal now was to survive the descent.

After four hours, we finally reached the Balcony—a tiny piece of level ground at 8,430 meters the size of two double beds. More than twenty-five climbers were clambering precariously around this staging post looking for their oxygen stashes, changing tanks, eating snacks, and hydrating. There wasn't a safety rope in sight, and all around us were huge drop-offs. We were like a bunch of penguins fighting to stand on the same piece of narrow ice, enveloped by danger. If David Attenborough ever wanted to do a series on Everest and human behavior, he'd definitely want to catch this moment.

Within this circus of chaos, I pulled off my mask and tried to break off the ice that had formed around my oxygen regulator valve. I was still unhappy with the flow of oxygen and wondered if my exhaustion was due to a faulty valve, causing my tank oxygen to mix with the outside air and dilute my intake. Regardless, it was too late to fix it. When I turned around, I couldn't find the rest of the team. Being separated from my team at this crucial juncture made me suddenly feel like a three-year-old boy lost in a shopping mall. Luckily, my brain refired itself and I remembered to look for the reflectors Scott had given us. I immediately picked out the rest of the team. Scott's anal focus on details, which could be so annoying at Base Camp, suddenly came into its own now. Details matter when your life is on the line.

After twenty minutes at the Balcony and with a fresh tank of oxygen, we left and headed up the eastern ridge. As we crossed a massive and exposed shoulder of snow and ice, the clear sky enveloped us, the stars and reflective light creating a monochrome twilight backdrop. There were no sounds to be heard other than boots and crampons piercing the snow. It was like the mountain itself was holding its breath and allowing us to pass, and we were slowly moving through. Each step felt like a Herculean effort as we continued deeper into the Death Zone.

I fell into a trancelike state, walking on autopilot, focused on my steps, unclipping and reclipping at the fixed-line anchors. This worked well for an hour until the line ground to a crawl and then to a complete halt. Here the air was colder and the breeze stiffer than the sheltered gullies from earlier. My feet began to get cold. The subzero breeze cut at my face. And my brain shifted its focus from steady progress to valid concerns, mainly: (1) my oxygen supply and whether I would have enough of it and (2) the impact the cold could have on my stationary body.

After thirty minutes, my toes on both feet had moved from being cold to feeling like pins and needles and then to a throbbing pain. After another fifteen minutes, the pain was replaced by a sense of numbness. I could still move my toes, but I could no longer feel normal sensation in them. This was a clear sign of pending frostbite and a profoundly dangerous situation to be in at this height. I tried my best to wiggle them, but inside a hard plastic boot, there was little space to get much movement. My mind raced with thoughts of losing toes and having to learn to walk again without them. I tried to distract my mind by turning around and asking Ania and Bill how they were doing.

"Cold, very cold. My feet are not good," Ania said, physically shivering.

"Feeling chilly here and I hope we get moving soon, Vivian." Bill replied with his customary Colorado calmness. "How are your feet doing?"

There followed a succession of chats up and down our line asking one another how we were doing and then reaffirming advice to move our bodies to improve circulation, not just our toes. Blood circulation is a universal thing in the body, and moving one part will help other parts. Additionally, it was extremely important to drink water as dehydration impacts frostbite. Within minutes, my thoughts and fears were distracted by things to do. More subtly, we were reconnecting as a team in our difficult situation and helping one another.

On this exposed ridge of Everest, the nerve endings of my connections with my family were ever present. I thought of them back in Ireland, huddled in the kitchen of my parents' house. Every morsel of news would be discussed and consumed, the periods between updates creating a huge weight of worry, concern, and burden for them. They came into my mind regularly here on Everest—an energy and bond that busyness at sea level had a tendency to hide.

As the delay continued, my spirits slowly drained. How could we possibly make the summit with this speed of progress? With hope faltering in the darkness, I closed my eyes and replaced my situation with memories of time on a beach back home in the United States. The mental respite reduced the intensity of the shivers as my mind drifted off, but that made me feel colder.

When I finally opened my eyes, I saw a flicker of color

on the very edge of the horizon—initially light pink, then purple, before slowly melding into a fierce and glowing orange. It was just before 5:00 a.m.—we had been climbing for over eight hours, and sunrise was being released before us. Within minutes, what had been a black canvas with stars transformed into an illuminated landscape of color and contrast. We had climbed so high, I now noticed the soft bend of the horizon; for the first time in my life I could witness the curvature of the earth while standing on it. Below us, the entire population of the planet were going about their business: humanity tucked in their beds, at work, at school, or spending time with their families. We were earth's astronauts, above it all.

As rays of sunlight broke the horizon, lifting me from the despair of moments earlier, I felt a deep sense of appreciation. Not just for all I already had in this world but for the metaphor that this moment represented. Every single day of my life—all 29,200 days if I lived to 80—would have this same reset opportunity. Each day would be a chance to refresh, turn the page, and let go of the past—of burdens, ignorance, disagreements, pains, and setbacks—and acknowledge that I alone have control over my thoughts, how I feel, and my actions around others. I looked back down the line and saw my teammates' faces, their eyes similarly glistening at the sight before us. It was ironic to think we had come all this way—to the Death Zone—to feel alive.

The line started moving again soon after, and with that, combined with the rays of the sun touching our bodies, the sensation in my feet slowly came alive again. I now had a reverse experience: initially the sensation was of throbbing pain, then pins and needles, before finally a feeling of warmth from blood moving again. It had been an extremely close call.

As the sun rose, our situation and level of precariousness on that slope was revealed fully. We were above all other peaks and climbing the final vestiges of Everest's summit cone. Every cell in my body felt exposed. The 70-degree pitch of the slope itself was akin to the Lhotse Face. The steepness seemed absurd when the backdrop was nothing but sky. It felt like we were on sacred territory—above the weather and above where all forms of life could survive. On the right side were snow and packed ice, and on the left was exposed rock. We were choosing the much harder route: through the rock and away from the snow, which would have been infinitely easier to climb. My failing mind couldn't understand why until we had a delay and I asked Bill, who was behind me.

"That snow field is a huge avalanche risk, so we're avoiding it. Don't worry; the rocks aren't going anywhere. It's just us who have to hang on."

Toward the top of the ridge above us, the outcrop was similarly steep, and memories of the Yellow Band flooded back into my head. There was a significant bottleneck because climbers had to literally haul themselves up this steep rock and stretch/jump across a 1-meter (3.3-foot) gap, in crampons, at almost 8,700 meters. The rock was so steep and difficult that some Sherpa were perched on outcrops, motivating their exhausted team members while guiding their foot placements. Loose rock fragments the size of saucepans broke free, taking off down the side of the mountain. They could take you out, so you had to maintain hyper-situational awareness and listen for muffled shouts of "Rocks!"

When it was my turn, the first thing I noticed were the

frayed ropes to the side of our fixed line—remnants from previous years' expeditions, their colors bleached and threads split into hundreds of strands. Nothing survived in this place. The sun was rising quickly, and the light was incredibly strong. When I looked out over the horizon, I had to concentrate and squint to focus on the distance. An issue at extreme altitude, my body was redirecting oxygen from the extremities such as my eyes to my core internal organs.

I finally surmounted the ridge—each lift of my feet a slow, conscious, and draining effort. My eyes were angled downward at my boots as I noticed the ground leveling out. Lifting my gaze, a dramatic panoramic view opened up in front of me. We had reached the south summit of Everest. A dome-shaped peak of snow and ice on the southeast ridge, and just 100 meters below the actual summit, this subsidiary peak is still the second-highest peak in the world, even higher than Pakistan's infamous K2.

Heaving for breath and air that was not there, I pulled off my glasses, squinted my eyes, and focused on the sight before me. Straight ahead was the Hillary Step, the most famous and technically challenging obstacle on Everest—a terrifying, near-vertical rockface. A line of climbers on the rope hauled themselves up on the rock, swaying from side to side, their tenuous foot grips nearly impossible to maintain. Between me and the Hillary Step was the Cornice Traverse—an 80-meter-long knife-edge on a ridgeline. No more than one and a half boot widths across, it was like a balance beam, but the drop-offs on either side were stupendous. A misstep to the left would cause me to fall 2,400 meters down into Nepal, while a misstep to the right would send me 3,000 meters down the Kangshung Face into Tibet.

I felt a sharp, cold shock surge through my entire body

as reality hit me—fear, in its purest form. Every one of my senses suddenly rejected my being there and what lay ahead. The danger had become so exponential that it was impossible to ignore.

"I don't think I can do it, I don't think I can summit. I'm not feeling good . . . , " Scott said, leaning against a boulder.

"Vivian, are you okay?" Bill called loudly, squinting through the blowing ice crystals.

"No air, Bill, no air!" I replied.

"Stay here and change your oxygen for a fresh tank!"

Bill slowly moved away with other team members, heading toward the knife-edge. The remaining fumes of energy in my body evaporated as my mind grew darker, followed by an intense and piercing loneliness.

Why are you here? The unfamiliar voice came from deep inside, stripping me bare.

Why are you trying to prove how good you are? How smart you are? What a good son and brother you are? How successful you are? My mind was unraveling, and I felt vulnerability like I had never experienced before.

Why are you here? These four words repeated themselves incessantly.

The ego was of no use to me. The persona was of no use to me. I was alone with my truth.

I had read books about the mountaineering greats who had been here before me (Hillary, Norgay, and Messner) and of those greats who never made it home (Mallory, Hall, and Fischer, to name a few). Rob Hall's body lay just a few meters from where I was standing. They were so much more experienced and accomplished than I was on that mountain. All of those people had a clear mind as to why they were there. They had purpose. I felt like an imposter here, one without inner purpose—the worst kind.

Perhaps the most painful feeling was that I was not able to change my reality. I was there, exhausted, totally spent, and I would die leaning against this rock with this reckoning filling my head until my last breath. I didn't come here to die, yet here I was. The ultimate question would be what I would leave behind to those I cared about or served as an example to—my family, friends, colleagues, clients, and society at large. Those who knew me would likely cheer at my list of achievements: hard work, grit, and toil against the odds. I would be seen as an architect and a builder, a beacon of doing it "My Way." I could imagine Sinatra's song filling the soliloquy. But it felt empty—a hollow husk with no core.

The question that mattered was not so much how they would remember me, but how I made them feel. Would they remember me just "doing things," or had I penetrated their souls and made them feel better about themselves? I knew the answer: "Not enough." I was chasing dreams without leaving an impression inside people.

I had never felt so lonely in my entire life.

Welling tears broke like a dam and ran down my cheeks before quickly freezing. I closed my eyes in self-pity and shame. My wet eyelids quickly froze, further restricting any escape. I was going back into my inner cave to lie in the bed I had made myself over my thirty-nine years. That would be my legacy. The only thing I could hope for before dying, right then and there, was to make peace with myself.

I'm not sure where my thoughts disappeared to next. I only remember suddenly seeing my late brother, Paul, in my mind. He was standing next to me, his smiling nineteen-year-old face bright against the backdrop of the sky. The mountain no longer existed. He reached out his hand,

and I grabbed it tightly. The noise in my mind quieted. The heaviness on my chest evaporated. My heart filled with peace until I felt ready for what was to come next. He was taking me with him.

I don't know how long that moment lasted. It felt like an extended amount of time, though likely it was not.

A real hand touch my shoulder.

I rubbed my eyes, breaking the frozen tears, and opened them to see Gomba, one of our Sherpa.

"Mr. Vivian, how are you?" he asked.

I stared blankly at him.

He leaned in and pulled my face close to his tanned and weathered face, filling my view. "Mr. Vivian, we cannot stay here. We stay, we both die. We must go now." His deep brown eyes penetrated my soul. "Follow me, Mr. Vivian, follow me." I could feel the strength of this man before me, and I surrendered.

He changed out my oxygen tank and we left the South Summit. Scott was no longer at the rock, and as I looked upward I could see his outline ahead of me. The only thing I had in my mind was to follow Gomba's boot steps. Where he put his left boot, I followed with my left boot. The same with the right boot, then the left, again, and so on. I had surrendered fully to this man and believed in him implicitly.

I have no recollection of crossing the knife-edge, only the view of each boot step. What woke me up were his boots scraping and sliding on steep rock as he hauled himself up. We were in the middle of the near-vertical Hillary Step before I realized Gomba was taking me up, not down! I refocused my mind and followed his placements to the exact detail. Where he slid, I slid, but more importantly, where his boot took hold, so did mine.

As we slowly inched our way upward, I heard voices. I looked up and, to my surprise, saw a line of climbers coming down the same rope. They had summited and were descending. With thousands of meters of just air and space all around us, and the valleys distant below, it was incredibly dangerous. Clipping on and off the rope to pass me, they navigated the near-vertical rock. At least the process slowed us down, and I was able to rest between the steps.

Near the top of the Hillary Step, there was just one huge boulder left in the way. It had a smooth dome shape and couldn't be climbed around. I hauled myself up as far as I could go and then lunged with all my strength until I managed to sit on the top of its dome. Facing the wrong way, I had to pirouette 180 degrees to be able to continue. My hands shook uncontrollably. It felt like I was sitting on top of the Empire State Building, sheer exposure all around me, but with eight times the height of a fall should I slip. I moved in slow motion, imagining my butt was stuck to the rock, while I swung my legs over the abyss. I took my time until I had turned fully.

With the Hillary Step behind me, I made my way up the last snow-covered slope leading toward the summit—steep but a sanctuary compared to what I had climbed moments before. The 300 meters seemed to go on forever. The hardpacked ice and snow under my feet crackled from my crampons. My eyes locked in position, tracking one boot after the other. Finally, and unexpectedly, it flattened out into a space no larger than the size of a bed. I unclipped from the rope. At 9:23 a.m. on May 23, thirteen hours after leaving the South Col, I had reached the summit of the highest point on earth. At 8,848 meters (29,029 feet), I could go no higher.

I embraced Gomba. He had believed in me when I had lost all faith in myself. He had led me through the most difficult obstacles selflessly. I committed to never forgetting that man and what I learned from him. I then embraced my teammates, who were already celebrating. Their faces were ecstatic with excitement as they smiled and shouted through the thinnest air on the planet. I didn't feel anything apart from numbness physically and emotionally.

I sat down on the mound of prayer flags. This was definitely not the appropriate thing to do, but my legs gave way, and I no longer had control over them. The expression on my face must have said it all. I was exposing teeth and forcing a smile, but it was really more a grimace of pain. I took off my gloves briefly and rummaged in my bag before pulling out the large, laminated card naming the charity I had raised money for, and Bill took a photo. Part of my exhausted brain wanted people who had donated to my cause to know I had reached this physical goal. It was an automatic reaction without any thought given. I felt my fingers on my right hand get cold within seconds. I tried to warm them up again but a strange feeling remained.

I looked out, and all around me it appeared as if I were standing on the sky itself. There was nothing above me and nothing beside me. Sagarmatha—Everest—was part of the sky itself. The curvature of the horizon meant I was standing on the roof of the earth. There were no words for me to utter. I was just captivated by the moment of being here. I felt empty and hollow, but somehow in a positive way. The black cloud had lifted, and there were no longer judgmental and negative voices running through my head, just a vacuum that the numbness represented. It was an amazing feeling to be here, even if I didn't know *why* I was here.

I stayed at the summit all of fifteen minutes before it was time to leave. One advantage of my delay at the South Summit and subsequently passing the trail of descending climbers was that the crowd had cleared, and it felt as if our team members were the only ones left at the summit. That in and of itself made it an incredible moment. I felt a deep sense of pride and, above all, a heartfelt connection with those people with whom I had shared so much to get here. We were family now.

As I surveyed the view one last time, I noticed a large bank of clouds coming in from the east. The wind was picking up strength. I immediately thought of the cyclone. It was time to go home. It would take two full days to get back to Base Camp, which would be the most dangerous part of the expedition, when 80 percent of accidents tend to happen. Exhausted bodies and minds navigating steep descents is a recipe for disaster.

My legs were shaking as I stood up and slowly started down the trail. I kept it together until I approached the Cornice knife-edge—the part I had no recollection of crossing just a couple of hours earlier. I looked out in front of me and saw the scale of the obstacle—the knife-edge ridge, the huge drop-offs on either side. With the ever-increasing clouds, the sun was starting to flicker as it faded. The soft breeze on the summit had turned into small gusts of wind. I stepped out onto the tiniest of trails, balancing like a gymnast on the beam at the Olympics. The trail was only slightly wider than one boot. To get the other boot ahead of the first, the trick was to swing the other leg around to the front but avoid catching my crampon in my gear. If I made one mistake, it was so ridiculously far to fall that a dark part of my brain imagined I would have time to make a last phone call mid-air before impact. My legs were shaking, then my body as well. Ahead of me, Scott looked around.

"Keep it together," he shouted.

"I'm fine," I replied.

"You don't look fine!"

I shook and wobbled the whole way across the knife-edge, but I survived to continue down the mountain.

At a break soon after, Scott started lecturing me about the danger of not holding concentration. His tone was terse and condescending. I listened quietly as I peeled back the wrapper on my snack bar until I couldn't take it anymore.

"Listen, I'm doing the fucking best I can. I got up this thing and I'm going to get down. I'm not choosing my legs to shake. They are doing that all on their own. Trust me that I'm going to get down safely, and if you're going to say something, say something that fucking motivates me!" It was an eruption of a lot of stuff. Only I knew what I had gone through on the way up and the demons I had faced. I just couldn't take a lecture in that moment.

He stared back at me without saying a word, completely taken aback. As a leader, Scott was exceptional in so many ways, but at times he relied on the hammer more than the carrot. That was fine when mixed with his wisdom, things to learn, and our sheer excitement of climbing up. But at that later stage of the journey, I needed something else. I needed encouragement, not judgment, and as a result he got an Irish blast in the Death Zone. I think it also served as some sort of release for me as I continued down with a clearer head and slightly less wobbly legs.

Delays increased the farther we descended as climbers ahead of us created bottlenecks, sitting on the trail, exhausted and delirious. Their Sherpa tried to motivate them to continue while coordinating on radios with the rest of their teams. The technique required to ascend was completely different from the strategy to descend. There were parts where we had to abseil and other areas where we would arm wrap (wrap the rope around one arm to provide support as we slowly dropped down the rocks) as we walked down the steep slopes face-first. Upon reaching the Balcony, there was a buildup of people. When I arrived, Scott and others were standing around a climber who was very ill. Clearly suffering from pulmonary edema, he was pale, barely conscious, and his lips had turned bluish in color. Scott helped by giving him oxygen and assigning one of our Sherpa to help him in his descent to the South Col/Camp 4.

Soon after the Balcony, I became separated from the team, and my already weakened state grew worse. The tips of my fingers on my right hand were tingling, and I knew I had done some tissue damage on the summit when I had briefly taken off my gloves. The big question was whether it would get worse over time or remain at that level. The weather was deteriorating rapidly, and it was snowing steadily in a blustery wind, limiting visibility to no more than 30 meters.

At the next anchor point, I sat down in the snow and put my head in my hands. *How could this be? I was coming down the mountain so surely this must be easier?* I thought. Unhitching my backpack, I checked my oxygen flow and realized that my tank was completely empty. I was effectively without oxygen in the Death Zone. I couldn't see anything in the whiteout other than the rope of the fixed line, so I just continued until each anchor point (every 50 meters) and then sat down to catch my breath and absorb whatever little oxygen was in the atmosphere. It was an incredibly debilitating feeling—to know that not even gravity can make up for a lack of oxygen. Stories of climbers no longer being able to move 100 meters short of camp now made complete sense. I was running on fumes.

Finally, after more than twenty hours, I saw a flicker of color through the blizzard, and Camp 4 appeared before me. It took me more than thirty minutes to walk the last 200 meters and reach the South Col. I had to rest four times. Camp 4 was like an oasis, the first remotely flat and safe area I had seen since we left the night before. I unzipped our tent and peered inside. Ania was stretched out in her sleeping bag, her eyes staring upward. She, too, was totally spent. We hugged tightly before mumbling briefly about what we had gone through.

She was staring at me with a furrowed brow for some moments before exclaiming in typical Polish style, "Vivian, you look wrecked, and your face is unrecognizable."

I smiled. "You're not exactly looking like the Mona Lisa yourself there." We both burst into weak laughter. It was the first time I'd laughed in days, and my lungs hurt from the exertion.

We took photos of each other to bear testament to what we had been through. My face was swollen, my lips were destroyed, and my cheeks and forehead were sunburned to a cinder, but it was my eyes that held the full truth. They were completely bloodshot, and my eyelids were swollen. Most obvious of all, they were empty and hollow. Trauma and shock were in them, as if I had witnessed a terrible event that had permeated my soul. It had been the longest day in my life. My D-Day.

Soon after, as if on cue, a Sherpa appeared at our tent

with hot tea, followed by more hot water and ramen. As we slowly tried to swallow our first meal in twenty-four hours, the deteriorating weather progressed into a storm, wind and driving snow battering the tent. I assessed my fingers and the tingling was the same. Bill came to check on us, and we agreed it looked like I had what's called "frostnip," the stage just before frostbite. I would likely recover, but it would limit my rope handling ability on the way down.

After eating, I crawled into my sleeping bag, adjusted my oxygen mask to tap into my new supply, which Gomba brought me, and promptly fell into a comatose-like sleep. There were no dreams—my unconscious mind fully surrendered. In an odd way, I felt safe there on the South Col. It was the longest uninterrupted sleep I had had in six weeks.

At 6:00 a.m. I slowly started waking up, but I couldn't open my eyes. Panic set in—was I still in a dream? It didn't feel like it. Was I even alive? Maybe something happened in the night, and I didn't make it. My mind was groggy, but my heart was racing. I pulled my hands out of the sleeping bag and felt my eyelids. There was a crust of dried pus on them. I carefully rubbed them, and the crusts broke off. Slowly I was able to open my left eye, then my right. The tent zip hadn't been fully closed and the blizzard overnight had blasted snow in through the small opening. It was completely white with at least two centimeters of snow on everything. Ania lay motionless. Her eyebrows were completely white with snow, which had also encased her hair and her entire sleeping bag. I wasn't sure if she were alive. I called out to her. Nothing. I called out again. Nothing. My heart rate exploded. I tried a third time by tapping her shoulder. Eventually, she moaned and slowly woke up. We were okay.

We left camp in a light blizzard and slowly made our

way back down the mountain toward Camp 2. As the hours passed, the snow became heavier. Visibility dropped to no more than 5 to 7 meters. As we came to the Geneva Spur and moved into our abseil routines (it was too steep to climb down), we were in a whiteout, essentially blind. It was like being on the inside of a Ping-Pong ball, impossible to tell up from down or have any situational awareness. Our sight was our altitude meter, and without it we had to rely on our feet as our sensors and listen extremely carefully to our teammates. But in a blizzard, it's hard to differentiate which direction noises are coming from. That level of concentration in my condition was draining, and I ended up going into a trancelike meditative state of no thinking— just intuiting—to overcome the many dangers around us. Our experience and seasoning over the past month as a team were coming to the fore.

As usual, we were with our Sherpa team. Their strength and resilience continued to surprise and impress me. They were carrying up to 40 kilograms (90 pounds) of gear on each of their backs, including tents, used oxygen tanks, and supplies from Camps 3 and 4. My one searing memory is of my Sherpa, Gomba, with a massive pack on his back, taking a break at an anchor point on the Lhotse Face. Although clearly exhausted, he put his hand over his eyes in a salute pose, trying to see me through the driving snow to make sure I was okay. The Sherpa were our guardian angels and people of character, compassion, and resilience.

After six hours, just as we made it to the last part of the Lhotse Face, the blizzard cleared, and Camp 2 appeared like a mirage below us. Upon reaching the bottom of the near-vertical wall of ice, I felt a huge weight lift off my shoulders. I purposefully collapsed headfirst into a snow drift. Feeling the coolness of the snow against my sweating face, I screamed with delight, stretched out my arms and legs simultaneously, and made a snow angel to the applause of my team. I stood up, caked in snow from head to foot, and reverted to the six-year-old me. God, I had missed this kid!

As close as we had become during our expedition, my teammates had no idea how much emotional weight I was carrying with me on our summit day and what that feeling of relief meant to me. That's the notable thing about a journey like this: everyone is carrying their own feelings, burdens, and awakenings—both conscious and unconscious—but they aren't necessarily sharing them. In the best-case scenario, it can often take months or years for the full meaning to distill and allow people to talk freely and articulately about it.

All of our individual tents at Camp 2 had already been disassembled and taken down to Base Camp, so we were sharing the group tent for the afternoon and night. Taking off our boots collectively in this small living space was an eye-watering experience. After one week of close to zero hygiene, the pungent steam that rose could have resuscitated the dead. We looked like a bunch of dirty hippos in a pond—flailing around with complete exhaustion. Our bodies in varying degrees of physical breakdown, we compared injuries and damage, trying to outdo one another, while recovering our humor and good cheer. It was a moment of complete vulnerability, camaraderie, and childhood charm. What was always in us from birth was finally being lived and experienced again.

Hours later, as the light began to fade, Bill arrived back at camp, exhausted. He had been delayed helping to rescue a seriously ill British climber who was abandoned by his team and suffering from acute pulmonary edema. With the help of a Sherpa, they were able to carry the climber down to Camp 2, where a rescue helicopter then managed to land before flying the climber off the mountain. It was a dramatic end to another long and grueling day on the mountain, and we still had one more day to go.

After dinner, I borrowed the satellite phone, escaped our packed team tent, and stood outside under the sky. It was good to be alone. The storm had passed, and it was a perfectly clear night with a massive full moon perched in the sky between Everest and Lhotse. I had been thinking a lot about my family. They had likely received updates about our summit attempt through the Mountain Trip blog, which was tracking us as a team, but not from me personally. The last update was the voicemail I posted the afternoon before our summit attempt, so I knew they must be at their wits' end.

My hands shook as I dialed my parents' number. The phone crackled and pinged for what felt like forever. I imagined it going from satellite to earth and then rerouting onward to Europe. The line dropped twice before even connecting to Ireland. On the third dialing attempt, it went through and I heard the familiar Irish ring tone—*ring-ring*, break, *ring-ring*, break, *ring-ring*, and then a voice.

"Hello?" My dad's voice was strong, warm, and familiar.

I had my words already chosen but I couldn't speak. Instead, I broke down and cried—hard. Harder than I'd ever cried before in my life. He had been a tough father growing up, and I had always been somewhat distant from him. A high achiever himself and very family oriented, he had high expectations for his sons, was no-nonsense, didn't give praise, and rarely used the word *love*. He wanted us to be humble, strong, and always do our best in everything we did. He would share with others how very proud of us he was but would rarely tell us directly.

But on that mountain, after what I had just gone through, just hearing his voice, I felt the sacrifices he and my mother had made in their lives for me to be there. I was overpowered by emotion, and it represented two words: *family* and *love*. The emotional dam burst lasted a full minute and then, like a passing thunderstorm, the tears ended as quickly as they had started.

I filled my lungs with air, wiped my eyes, and calmly said, "Dad, how are you and Mum doing?"

"We're fine. How are you and where are you now?"

"I'm at Camp 2. We made it to the summit—the whole team."

"We are so very proud of you, Vivian!"

Tears rolled down my cheeks. "It was tough. I didn't think I'd make it. I wasn't sure I'd see you again. So happy to hear your voice right now. I love you both very much."

"We love you very much too." The call finished and I stood there for a few minutes looking at the moon and the star-drenched sky. I felt connected.

I spent half an hour outside in the clear air, taking stock of the moment and the emotion I had just felt. Part of me felt like I'd soiled myself by not being able to manage my emotions, that I was hijacked by something I could not control. Growing up in our family, emotions were not shown freely. I'd seen my Dad cry only twice in my entire life: when my great aunt (who lived with us) died and when my younger brother, Paul, died. Then, Dad's stoic and supremely alpha personality completely unraveled. He was rudderless, beside himself, and couldn't be consoled.

As the eldest of five children, he had been expected to

lead and become an example to his siblings when his mother died tragically at a young age. He lived his life with a burden on his shoulders. Living with a constant pressure always to be his best—for himself and his family—the biggest tool in his box was control. Control was his security blanket.

As I closed my eyes and breathed in the crisp and fresh Himalayan air, for the first time I recognized a separation between how I had been brought up and who I was. The Everest journey I was on harnessed control as a tool to achieve the achievable, the necessary, but it was never to be ruled blindly by it. Those who had done that became detached from reality and absorbed much higher risk. Control was powerful, but it had to have guide rails.

I returned to the main tent, where the whole team of climbers and guides slept together on the floor in our sleeping bags. This group of people had become my family, and I felt a deep connection with them. I was physically and emotionally wiped and slept deeply. The intensity of the past six weeks, like permafrost, was beginning to thaw.

The alarm went off at 2:00 a.m. and we gathered our remaining gear for one final descent through the Western Cwm and the Khumbu Icefall. Reaching the top of the Icefall just after dawn had broken, I imagined I could smell the potato fries from Base Camp and leaned into the descent with gusto. The Icefall had transformed itself yet again. It was unrecognizable and more dangerous than ever. The crevasses had widened, and toward the end of the climb there was a ladder bridge almost 8 meters across, made up of four ladders strapped together with twine. I surveyed it, but the fear was gone. I launched myself onto the aluminum rungs, feeling the swaying and bounciness almost immediately, but my heart rate didn't move a beat. I had found peace. My body and mind, through exhaustion and trauma, had found trust in the other. I felt whole for the first time in a long while.

When we came out of the Icefall, we found a group of our Sherpa waiting just below us on the glacier. Our Base Camp "Welcoming Committee" stood clapping as we reached them. They had drinks, tea, and freshly baked snacks and unfurled a banner they had made themselves, adorned with drawings and the following words:

Welcome to Bescamp
Mountain Trip Team
Heartly Congartulation
Sucsessful Everest Expedition 23rd May 2010

The effort they put into creating that sign for us, in a language not their own, represented everything they stood for and how they lived: being their best, together. It was beautiful and deeply meaningful. These people had supported us, cared for us, cooked for us, and kept us alive, sharing in our success.

Walking into Base Camp to the sound of Michael Jackson's "Thriller" on the camp speakers added to the high. How appropriate, I thought—the past week had traumatic moments, where, like in the song, the soul of this man woke from its slumber. My aching body grooved to the rhythm, and before long we had a spontaneous Sherpa-climber dance party going at 10:30 a.m.

At Base Camp I called my family again to let them know that I was finally completely safe. As I was just about to finish the call, a family member said, "Vivian, I heard from Dad that you said you had a very rough summit day and almost didn't make it, and you thought you wouldn't make it down. Listen, this doesn't matter, and you don't have to tell people that part. You reached the top of the highest mountain on earth, and you came down safely. That's what matters, and it is the only story you need to share."

The words stung, and my reply was immediate and instinctual. "You have no idea what I went through up there, and I'm not blaming you for that—how could you possibly know? But you need to understand that the truth, the suffering, the questions, and the way I felt up there *is* the story, and I will proudly share it with every person who's willing to hear it."

It must have felt like an overreaction to them—an exhausted man with a tired mind. In reality, it was quite the opposite. My mind was crystal clear on that answer. It was so unusual for me to feel that way—I love my family, and normally I would have little reaction to any one of them sharing their advice and views about any topic. But this time it was different, and I took the advice personally. I had not come off that mountain the same man as when I arrived almost two months ago, and that was a point of humility and pride.

I was born and grew up in the Republic of Ireland, an island off the western tip of Europe and a former colony of the British Empire, where people historically had lower confidence and were overly concerned with what other people thought of them. Being positive and portraying our best sides, always, was a natural disposition. Although I still loved this country of my birth very much, and it had changed so much for the better over the years since I had been away, perhaps these traits, like a chip on my shoulder, still remained and would take a little longer to grow out of.

That night, our exceptional and resourceful chef, Surki, created a feast for us, over which we spent hours talking, laughing, and sharing stories. Toward the end of dinner, the entire Sherpa team came into the tent and we celebrated together with Nepalese music blaring and spontaneous Sherpa dancing. Initially, everybody joined in on the electric atmosphere, but after some time something interesting happened. The Western climbers, including me, stood back and just watched the Sherpa, in awe of these incredible people. Most of them had not been near the summit, and many had been supporting our camps, yet here they were smiling from ear to ear and laughing from the depths of their bellies. They understood that our success was also theirs.

As a Westerner, it was a moment to appreciate how working incredibly hard toward common goals in an environment of laughter while also being deeply present throughout the experience was entirely possible. Looking at those faces, we were the ones who were learning from them. They had the greater inner strength, inner peace, and respect for their community and natural environment. As I stood watching that precious moment, I thought only of how I could possibly capture this *way of being* inside my own self and bring it home with me—living and laughing like a Sherpa.

The following morning we had breakfast and witnessed the dismantling of Base Camp and the lines of yaks awaiting their loads before retreating down the mountain. The camp was being unbuilt for another year, and the area would soon return to its natural state for the brutal monsoon season. Another chapter about that relatively recently climbable mountain was over.

Instead of enduring a three-day trek back down the valley all the way to the airport in Lukla, we decided to pool our dollars and pay for a helicopter to take us on the fifteen-minute flight to the narrow landing strip we had arrived on. Excitement was reaching a crescendo as we heard the engine and blade turns from above, but Everest held one final lesson for us.

As the helicopter dropped altitude to land, we readied ourselves to run toward it. However, the pilot started waving us back with his arms. We stopped and stood with puzzled faces. Perhaps there was a technical problem. Soon after it landed, the reason became unnervingly clear. A small group of Sherpa ran to the passenger cabin of the helicopter and retrieved a stretcher wrapped in a blanket. It was the body of the climber from Kazakhstan who had perished the year before in an avalanche at Camp 2. They finally had an opportunity to retrieve the body and lay the soul of this climber to rest.

Moments later we climbed into the helicopter. It was a surreal experience. For almost two months, every inch I had moved was an effort to make it here. For the first time, I could relax and not feel my muscles for a while. We rose and turned down the mountain, gradually leaving the Khumbu glacier behind. We retraced our steps all the way back toward Lukla. With the valleys gradually increasing in color and foliage toward a vibrant and verdant green below, I thought of how fine a line life actually represents. Our dreams and aspirations, equally exciting and motivating, are just one side of the coin. The other side is that we don't know what the next moment will bring. Life can change in an instant. We live in a moment, and that is the only thing we have control over. Right here, right now.

It's not the mountain we conquer, but ourselves.
—EDMUND HILLARY

Many people proudly declare that they or humankind have conquered Everest and, indeed, nature itself. My view is the opposite. Everest can never be conquered. Instead, the mountain itself serves as a metaphor for life. To conquer is to live through an ego, which misses the very essence of what an experience represents: to let go and live with vulnerability and recognize the strength that this entails; to revert to childlike curiosity and openness; to ask for help; and embrace the unknown and the change that comes with this, yet all the while to feel alive and recognize the strength that this *way of being* embodies—that is the true meaning of life and, ultimately, legacy.

The summit rotation was, in many ways, symbolic of the circle of life. A start and an end, with so many uncontrollables along the way. Choices to make, not just in actions but in the thoughts and emotions I allowed in my head and, above all, understanding their meaning and deciphering whether they were truly mine.

For most of us, life can feel like an unconscious ride on a roller coaster, as if we are perched on some track that moves us along with little or no control. In fact, the reality is different. While we don't have control over some things, these are the minority. For the most part, we allow ourselves to be prisoners of our habits, our conditioning, and our emotions. In a real sense, we are racing through life blindly at what feels like the speed of light, which is the one thing most people would like to change: to have more time, to slow it down, to be able to enjoy more, and to have more experiences.

Yet in order to do just that, we have to change ourselves— to get off the roller coaster. We need to take ownership of our awareness and become accountable to get past ourselves. It's about letting go, not taking on more. It's about simplifying rather than making things more complex. It's about presence of mind rather than action of mind.

Each morning, dawn breaks and represents a chance to

reset—to unshackle the past, to reduce any busyness that serves no purpose, to not feel like you have to constantly prove yourself. At its core, it's an opportunity to be closer to who you were born to be, move others in the process, and leave a ding on the universe.

And it begins with just one first step.

EPILOGUE

THE RETURN to civilization was a bumpy one. I caught a stomach bug during the descent from the summit and lost additional kilos of weight from my almost emaciated frame. After arriving in Kathmandu, I realized we were ahead of schedule by several days and decided that rather than push forward my eighteen hours of flights to get home sooner, I would use those days to try to recover. I would treat myself.

After our celebratory team dinner, I booked what ended up being a somewhat dated hotel/country club on the outskirts of Kathmandu. It had few guests and I felt completely at home. I had been with the same people day in and day out for almost two months and craved time alone.

The hotel had apparently once hosted the Nepal Masters Golf tournament, although its heydays were long gone. It had an ornate and luxurious garden and was surrounded by a rainforest. The strength of the colors overwhelmed me. My eyes had become numbed by the colors associated with snow, rock, and ice for so long, and here a full palette of color was revealed again. I looked at the garden like an astronaut looking back at earth, dazzled and humbled.

My first meal was another experience, when my senses of smell and taste finally returned. Sinking my teeth into that first steak, the first fresh vegetable, and the piece of fruit—nirvana. After a night of deep sleep in a massive bed, I put on a robe and walked down to the spa.

"Namaste," the staff beamed. "Sir, what treatment would you like today?"

I took a breath and quietly replied, "Just fix this broken body, please."

My stomach bug was symptomatic of my weakened immune system, and it took almost a month to finally clear the infection. The frostnip healed after about a month as well, and full feeling returned to my fingers. It took me three months to regain the weight I lost on Everest. My memory was impacted for almost six months due to the deficit of oxygen for such an extended period. Not dramatically, but enough for me to notice something was not right.

My return to New York City was a surreal experience. Walking through the throngs of people in the streets, looking stressed and caught up in the energy that is uniquely New York, I noticed myself smiling and feeling separated from everything that was happening around me. It was as if the busyness drug no longer had a hold on me. I felt in control to be myself, and it made me feel lighter, as if a weight had been lifted off my shoulders. My life had flashed before me so many times on Everest; I was appreciative of every single thing I had taken for granted before.

People always ask me, "What's the one thing you learned from climbing Mount Everest?"

It's difficult to name one specific thing. It represents many things to me: vulnerability, humility, intuition, legacy, compassion. Of course, I realize that not everyone will climb Mount Everest. But I believe that we each have our own *personal* Everest to climb. And it's different for everyone. It could be a challenge, a bereavement, a setback, or some dream or ambition that seems just beyond our reach, perhaps even ridiculous. This is your own Seventh Summit. But if you dig down very deep, I think you'll find, just as I did, that you already have all the resources you need inside you. You just need to "get on the plane."

Glossary

abseil. Descend a near-vertical surface by using a doubled rope coiled around the body and fixed at a higher point; alternatively known as *rappel.*

ascender. A mechanical device used for directly ascending a rope that slides freely up a rope but grips/locks when downward pressure is applied (helps arrest a fall).

cache. A supply of food, fuel, or equipment to be used at a future point in time.

Chomolungma. The Tibetan name for Mount Everest; its meaning is "Goddess Mother of the World."

chorten. An altar or a shrine structure for Buddhist offerings.

col. The lowest point or pass on a mountain ridge between two peaks.

cornice. An overhanging edge of snow or ice on a ridge or crest of a mountain, typically formed by wind.

crampon. A steel frame with sharp points/spikes that is attached to the bottom of a boot to make walking on hardpacked snow or ice easier.

crevasse. A deep crack or fracture/fissure found in an ice sheet or glacier, which can be up to 45 meters deep (150 feet).

189

fixed line. The practice of fixing in place anchored ropes to assist climbers on steep or icy sections of a route.

Gamow bag. A portable pressurized bag resembling a human-size cigar tube that combats the effects of acute mountain sickness by artificially creating the air pressure of a lower altitude.

glacial moraine. An accumulation of rocks and debris that has fallen onto the glacier surface or have been pushed along by the glacier as it moves.

High Altitude Cerebral Edema (HACE). A condition characterized by the buildup of excess fluid in the brain.

Ice Doctors. A team of highly skilled Sherpa deployed during the Everest climbing season to assist navigation through the Khumbu Icefall.

ice screw. A threaded tubular screw used on steep ice surfaces to hold a climber in the event of a fall. The screw becomes an anchor point, commonly used on fixed lines.

icefall. A portion of a glacier denoted by a relatively rapid flow and chaotic crevassed surface, caused in part by gravity, where there is a drop in height.

khata. A traditional Tibetan silk scarf given to visitors, symbolizing welcome and conferring good luck.

lama. A spiritual leader in Tibetan Buddhism.

Lhotse Face. A near-vertical icy slope located between Camp 2 and Camp 4.

puja. A ceremony at Base Camp asking the gods for permission to climb and for safe keeping. The ceremony is orchestrated by the Sherpa with the assistance of a lama.

Sagarmatha. The Sanskrit name for Everest, meaning "Peak of Heaven."

serac. A huge pillar or block of ice formed where crevasses intersect/meet.

Sherpa. One of the Tibetan ethnic groups native to the most mountainous regions of Nepal in the Himalayas. They are famed for their skills in mountaineering and in providing local support for climbers attempting peaks in Nepal.

snow blindness. A painful state that comes from the sun burning your eye cornea. It occurs if you don't wear suitable eye protection at altitude.

stupa. A mound or structure symbolizing the Buddha and his enlightened mind and presence.

yak. A long-haired work animal of mountain regions that are largely inaccessible to other types of transport animal. Related to bison and cattle, this ancient breed is well suited to high altitudes.

About the Author

VIVIAN JAMES RIGNEY is President and CEO of Inside Us LLC, a boutique executive coaching consultancy operating throughout five continents. He has helped implement leadership development initiatives for some of the world's leading companies and their executive teams.

The quest for personal success can often be a lonely journey. As an executive coach, Vivian becomes a trusted partner, known for building strong rapport and asking tough, incisive questions, with an uncanny ability to help people reveal the best version of themselves.

A graduate of École Nationale Des Ponts et Chaussées in Paris, he is a renowned speaker and expert on mindset and behavior, whose talks and presentations have inspired audiences globally. A native of Ireland, he has lived in the U.K., Germany, South Africa, France, and Finland and currently resides in New York City.

You can follow Vivian at
www.VivianJamesRigney.com.